PROMPT ENGINEERING FOR BUSINESS SUCCESS

AI PLAYBOOK TO SAVE TIME, BOOST PRODUCTIVITY, AND GROW YOUR CAREER

CAMERON BANKS

PROMPT ENGINEERING FOR BUSINESS SUCCESS

CAMERON BANKS

Copyright © 2025 by Synast Publishing

Published by Synast Publishing

ISBN: 978-1-968418-41-0

INTRODUCTION

In today's rapidly evolving business landscape, the integration of artificial intelligence is no longer a question of if, but when and how effectively it can be harnessed. Business leaders are faced with the pressing challenge of leveraging AI to not only maintain competitiveness but to drive substantial growth and innovation. This book is crafted to address these very needs by providing a comprehensive guide to prompt engineering, a pivotal skill that transforms AI from a technical tool into a strategic business asset.

Prompt engineering is the art of crafting precise instructions that enable AI systems to produce valuable and actionable business outcomes. It is akin to writing a compelling email subject line that demands attention or devising a strategic plan that aligns with company goals. Unlike traditional programming, prompt engineering requires an understanding of context, tone, intent, and the specific objectives of a business task. This book demystifies the concept, presenting it as a business skill accessible to all professionals, not just those with technical expertise.

The intended audience for this playbook includes business executives, managers, and professionals across various departments who are eager to unlock the potential of AI to enhance productivity, streamline operations, and foster career growth. The promise of this book is clear: to equip readers with the tools and knowledge necessary to implement prompt engineering effectively, thereby saving time, boosting productivity, and ultimately driving career advancement.

Readers will find a wealth of actionable insights, including step-by-step methods for crafting precise prompts, selecting the right AI tools, and integrating these into their daily workflows. The book also addresses common objections and misconceptions, positioning itself as a unique resource in a crowded market by offering a practical, business-first approach to AI.

This book serves as a roadmap, guiding readers through the essential concepts of prompt engineering with real-world examples, templates, and frameworks that are ready to implement across departments such as marketing, sales, HR, and operations. By the end, readers will be equipped with the confidence and competence to harness AI's transformative power, ensuring their business not only survives but thrives in the digital age.

CONTENTS

INTRODUCTION 1

Introduction to Prompt Engineering 7

Understanding the Basics.. 7

The Role of AI in Business 9

Why Prompt Engineering Matters 12

Setting the Stage for Success 14

Crafting Effective Prompts................................... 18

Elements of a Good Prompt................................. 18

Common Pitfalls and How to Avoid Them 20

Examples of Successful Prompts 22

Iterative Improvement 25

Integrating Prompt Engineering into Business............. 28

Aligning with Business Goals................................ 28

Cross-functional Collaboration............................. 31

Adapting to Change.. 33

Measuring Success 36

Building a Prompt Engineering Team 39

Identifying Key Skills.. 39

Training and Development 41

Creating a Collaborative Environment.................. 44

Leadership and Vision 47

Tools and Technologies 50

Choosing the Right Tools 50

Integrating with Existing Systems........................52

Staying Up-to-date..55

Security and Compliance 57

Developing Prompt Libraries..........................61

Creating Standardized Templates.........................61

Ensuring Consistency and Quality.......................63

Updating and Maintaining Libraries 66

Sharing Across the Organization 68

Case Studies of Success...................................72

Retail and E-commerce 72

Finance and Banking..75

Healthcare and Pharmaceuticals...........................77

Technology and Startups..80

Ethics and Compliance 83

Understanding Ethical Considerations.................83

Implementing Compliance Measures 85

Balancing Innovation and Regulation 88

Case Studies in Ethical Prompt Engineering 91

Future Trends in Prompt Engineering 94

Emerging Technologies 94

Predicting Industry Shifts 96

Preparing for the Future 99

Long-term Strategic Planning 101

Troubleshooting and Optimization 105

Common Issues and Solutions 105

Optimizing for Performance 107

Continuous Improvement 110

Feedback Loops 112

Prompt Engineering in Marketing 116

Crafting Persuasive Campaigns 116

Using AI for Market Analysis 118

Personalization at Scale 121

Tracking Marketing ROI 123

Prompt Engineering for Customer Support 126

Automating Responses 126

Improving Customer Satisfaction 128

Reducing Response Times 131

Measuring Support Success 133

Prompt Engineering for HR and Recruitment 137

Streamlining Hiring Processes 137

Enhancing Employee Engagement 140

Developing Training Programs 142

Monitoring HR Metrics 145

Conclusion and Call to Action 148

Recap of Key Points 148

Empowering Business Leaders.. 150

Next Steps for Implementation... 153

Looking Forward.. 156

EPILOGUE... 159

CHAPTER 1

INTRODUCTION TO PROMPT ENGINEERING

Understanding the Basics

In the world of modern business, AI has taken center stage in the way enterprises perform and compete in their businesses. An essential aspect of such technological revolution is prompt engineering, an ability that can address the human-machine intentional gap. The businesses can use AI to obtain valuable outcomes by creating fine-grained instructions.

In the most fundamental terms, prompt engineering is the art of coming up with clear, concise, and contextually relevant directions and instructing AI systems to complete tasks in the most effective way possible. Unlike conventional programming, whose knowledge demands are time-consuming, prompt engineering is more about gaining business contexts and aspirations. It is similar to writing the email subject line with the power to get attention and take action, but on a much bigger scale.

The importance of timely engineering is not related solely to the technical experience. It is a company-oriented skill that needs a strong comprehension of business goals, the specifics of communication, and the desired results. As an example, writing the prompt to have an AI write to a customer requires technical consideration of how to instruct the AI, as well as the tone, purpose, and business outcomes to align with.

This ability is utilized in many business situations: it may be used to write emails, summarize reports, and even automate customer service answers. In marketing, it can be used to create catchy content or personalize messages to the audience. In sales, it can help to personalize communication, and in operations, it can streamline operations by automating repetitive tasks.

It is essential to get an idea of the difference between prompts, templates, and frameworks. Prompts can be defined as the actual guidelines presented to the AI; a template is a kind of framework that gives predictions a certain structure, and frameworks are large-scale explanations of how to include prompts into business processes. To illustrate, a customer support template can have fields dedicated to having the names of customers and problem descriptions, thus providing a uniform and personal approach to customers.

Advancements in large language models (LLMs) such as GPT-3 and GPT-4 have increased the importance of prompt engineering. The models have crossed the threshold between being niceties and a necessity to conduct business, as they can carry out functions that result in a drastic increase in productivity and growth. The developments of the LLMs have played a critical role in ensuring that a timely engineering approach is essential to the businesses that wish to stay competitive.

There is no better time than now in this fast-moving business world to adopt prompt engineering. Prompt engineering: The ability to successfully use AI in business is a competitive advantage as digital transformation gains pace and automation becomes a core business strategy. The combination of AI and the preexisting systems, such as SaaS platforms, further increases the impact of AI, as the difference in adopting it for businesses is saving time and resources and optimizing service delivery.

In summary, it is paramount to know that the reasons why you need to get acquainted with the fundamentals of establishing prompt engineering, besides being a whole new skill, are that in the current climate of the use of artificial intelligence, businesses need tools in order to survive and get ahead of the competition. With the ability to expertly develop accurate prompts that will help companies achieve the synergies of efficiency, creativity, and innovation, corporates will be in a position to realise greater success in the new digital era.

The Role of AI in Business

Artificial Intelligence (AI) is already established as a business strategy staple, changing the ways businesses perform, innovate, and compete on a global scale. The fact is that its incorporation into business processes is not only a fashion but an essential move towards more intelligent and more efficient operations. The use of AI technologies will further automate routine functions and decision-making processes and provide customers with personalized experiences, thereby contributing to a significant boost in productivity and innovation.

Among the most significant effects that AI has on business is that it is able to process and analyse a tremendous amount of information and do it in record time. This allows businesses to understand information that could not be uncovered before or was too complicated to understand using conventional analytics tools. When businesses use machine learning algorithms, they are likely to be more accurate in predicting trends in the market, and knowing customers' likes and dislikes, as well as supply chain logistics. This evidence-based model will assist companies in making very important decisions that are crucial in sustaining competitive advantage.

In addition, AI is revolutionizing customer experience via chatbots and virtual assistants. These AI-based tools offer an uninterrupted customer service, receiving and solving complaints within a few minutes, which in turn improves customer satisfaction and the level of customer loyalty to a considerable extent. Automation of these interactions can help businesses lower the cost of a business operation without sacrificing service quality, as the savings cover operational expenditures, thus leaving human agents to focus on more complex tasks.

In marketing, AI is used to create more focused and practical campaigns. With predictive analytics, an AI system can pick out possible customer groups and tailor promotional content to address personal requirements and interests. This personalization helps to boost conversion rate, thus leading to better return on investment on marketing activities. Also, the AI can optimise ad placements and bidding as they occur, maximising the effectiveness of any marketing budget.

The contribution of AI in the business also involves the strengthening of product development processes. Using market data and customer feedback, AI systems can find market trends and gaps to dictate the plan to make new products that can satisfy the demand of the consumers. Not only does this ability shorten the time-to-market of new products, but it also puts these products at an advantageous position to succeed.

It also means that AI can be a catalyst for operational efficiency. In production, AI-powered robotics and automation processes will reduce production processes and enhance precision and quality management. In logistics, AI is used to optimize routes and inventories, which lowers costs and improves delivery times. These enhanced operational effectiveness brings down the costs substantially and maximizes profitability.

Nevertheless, the utilization of AI in the business aspect is not without its problems. Ethical issues like the privacy of data and the unfairness of AI code must be dealt with in order to adopt responsible usage. Businesses also have a responsibility to ensure the upskilling of their employees to work with AI technologies and develop a culture of continuous learning and adapting to change.

The role that AI plays in business in general is transformative, providing organizations with the prospect of newfound efficiency, innovation, and competitiveness. With the further development of AI technologies, their penetration into business strategies will only increase and further confirm their significance in achieving business success.

Why Prompt Engineering Matters

The importance of timely engineering in the fast-changing technological environment of business cannot be overemphasized. It is one of the key competencies in using the power of artificial intelligence to achieve business results. Prompt engineering itself is an artisanal skill that creates instructions that cause certain AI systems to generate outcomes that correspond to certain business objectives. This is not just a technical exercise but a strategic business operation, which has the potential to transform.

The major reason why productivity and efficiency give primary weight to prompt engineering is that they directly relate to it. In corporate environments where time is treated as equivalent to money, automating tasks with the use of AI-generated prompts results in a reduction in time spent. Some actions that have taken hours of human resources are now expedited to a few minutes, freeing up human resources to put their energy into other strategic initiatives. As another example, prompt engineering can be applied to eliminate the need for human operators to draft responses to frequently asked questions in customer service.

In addition, prompt engineering is used to improve the quality and regularity of outputs. Through careful prompt design, companies can make sure that AI systems give out not only accurate, but also consistent with their company brand voice and standards. This is especially true of marketing and communications, where one of the most important things is ensuring generality in tone and message so that brand integrity is maintained.

The other very strong argument in support of why timely engineering is so essential is that it provides a basis for innovation. Businesses can tap into new opportunities and dealings through the implementation of creative prompts. As an example, when it comes to product development, we can set AI on a task to provide innovative ideas according to the market environment and the feedback of the consumers, shortening the innovation cycle and providing enterprises with a competitive advantage.

Compliance and risk management are some of the most important requirements in the implementation of AI, and prompt engineering supports them as well. Businesses can reduce the risk of such AI-prompted problems as bias and data privacy by integrating compliance checks and ethical considerations into the prompts. Not only does this active approach save the company from any legal ramifications, but it also inoculates it against the suspicions of consumers who are now placing a greater emphasis on data protection and more ethical uses of AI.

In addition, timely engineering is essential in terms of the scalability of the business. As companies expand, there is an increased need to have scalable solutions. Prompt engineering allows companies to scale up their AI potential effectively, so that systems are able to process larger amounts of information and transactions without reducing their level of quality and speed.

In conclusion, timely engineering is the main principle of the contemporary business strategy. It makes operations more efficient, consistent, and of higher quality, improves risk management, and drives innovation. As companies move forward and embrace the use of AI in their business, prompt engineering tactics and skills will be ever more important, differentiating the companies that do well environmentally and financially from their competitors in the digital era.

Setting the Stage for Success

When it comes to business, it is important to take the right steps to establish a firm foundation so that it succeeds in the long run. Preliminary steps in any project usually determine the course and pace of the whole project. In terms of businesses that enter the innovative, yet complex sphere of on-time engineering, the only way to set the stage towards success is to understand both the opportunities and the constraints of artificial intelligence.

The bottom line in effective implementation is clarity of business objectives. Setting clear goals will make sure that AI-related endeavors are within the bigger picture of the corporation. This compatibility is essential because it streamlines resources and also maximizes the utility of AI applications. With a clear vision of the expectations of success, the business will develop well-targeted and effective prompt engineering strategies.

One of the techniques of integrating AI in business processes entails prioritizing the areas where AI could have the greatest impact on business processes. This needs an extensive review of current workflows in order to identify areas of inefficiency that AI can resolve. It can range from automating routine jobs to improving the decision-making process and personalizing the relationship with the customers, and it can go much further. Only when priorities are focused on areas that will yield the biggest returns on investments can success be achieved.

The foundations of success are laid in such a way that powerful structures and principles are put in place. These can be used as a blueprint for implementing AI in a manner that is sustainable and scalable. Creating specific playbooks that describe the aim, scope, and anticipated results of AI projects helps to improve the consistency of work of teams and departments. The frameworks also act as a means of knowledge transfer and allow successes to be duplicated in other parts of the business.

In addition to this, it is worth cultivating the culture of teamwork and lifelong learning. Promoting the collaboration of cross-departmental teams on AI projects will not only enlarge the field of innovation but also improve the quality of results. Frequent training and workshops ensure that teams are informed of current breakthroughs in AI and prompt engineering methodology. This method of continuous learning enables teams to experiment and iterate, resulting in more excellent and efficient solutions.

Establishing a powerful validation and feedback system is another crucial element in the process of achieving success. These processes include holding frequent reviews of the output of the AI to make sure that it conforms to the optimum grade of accuracy, relevance, and compliance. The addition of human oversight within AI processes allows companies to prevent the occurrence of mistakes and biases, therefore, preserving the quality and soundness of AI-generated results.

Lastly, a foray into prompt engineering will entail an embrace of ethical AI. Entrepreneurs must provide effective ethical principles of AI usage and ensure that all the implementations will be fair, transparent, and adherent to the business values. The commitment also works to mitigate any legal and reputational risks to the business, besides ensuring that the business gains trust among stakeholders and clients.

In a nutshell, pre-positioning success in prompt engineering is a careful combination of well-defined objective outlook, effective framework design, cooperative culture implementation, and ethical code-of-conduct compliance. By preconditioning this, businesses can unlock the potential of AI to spur innovation, efficiency, and growth, placing them on a trajectory of long-term success.

CHAPTER 2

CRAFTING EFFECTIVE PROMPTS

Elements of a Good Prompt

Designing a powerful prompt is comparable to laying the foundation of a building; it must be concise, straightforward, and intentional in nature to hold the edifice thereafter. There are important aspects that must be taken into consideration when coming up with prompts for AI solutions in business so that the desired results are achieved. A good prompt has the essence of taking abstract business goals and turning them into actionable tasks that artificial intelligence can go off and process.

It is important to be clear first and foremost. A prompt must formulate the task in clear terms without the possibility of misinterpretation. This is clarified by reporting in specific and concise terms that do not lack clarity. An example would be a less open prompt that said, "improve sales," as opposed to a more specific indication that would be to give a summary of last quarter sales data with key trends and areas of improvement. Not only does this inform what the AI should focus on, but it also constrains it to what that result should be.

The other pillar of an effective prompt includes contextual information. By providing background information, limitations, and expectations, AI can focus on more relevant answers. For example, when the task is to analyze market trends, data such as certain data points, time, and space scales might go a long way in helping AI fine-tune its results. Such situational layering guarantees that the responses given by the AI are based on the particulars of the business context where it should operate.

It is also important to define the output in terms of format and structure, regarding whether the feedback should follow the structure of a bulleted list, a detailed report, or a concise summary. The required form can be specified in this way, helping the AI to frame its/her response in accordance with the demands of the user. As an example, instructing the AI to "write the analysis in a three-paragraph executive summary" imposes a definite structure around which the AI can work.

The purpose of the prompt, i.e., intent, must be clearly stated. This is done by not only saying what to do, but also why. The awareness of the purpose of a task makes the AI prioritize the processes involved and concentrate on getting the output that is within business objectives. An example of this could be when the intent is to engage the customer deeper, then the prompt can tell the AI to "write a follow-up email to a client who attended one of our webinars." The intent in this context is vital as well as the actual task that the AI has to perform, dictating the tone and nature of its production.

Reinforcements such as exemplars or position-based instructions may also be added to the prompt. By explicitly specifying a role, like so, \"act as a customer support agent\". This will also impact the relevancy and suitability of the answers. Examples may be used to act as a benchmark for the AI and to show what the quality or form of output should look like.

Good prompting is an art that is dynamic and balanced between clarity, context, structure, and intent in wanting to achieve the complete benefit of AI in a business application. Carefully working on these components, business can ensure their AI functionality produces not only efficient but also strategically oriented outcomes.

Common Pitfalls and How to Avoid Them

The business world of today is a dynamic environment where staying clear of the many pitfalls of prompt engineering is important in a bid to realize business success. One of the major challenges is that of overgeneralization, in which prompts are not specific. Therefore, the output generated is not specific enough or is irrelevant to the business context. As a response to this, it is paramount that prompts are made so that the instructions are very clear and concise, and they are relevant to the determinants of the task they apply to. Restrictions and related business information assist in narrowing AI response so that it is in line with the business goals.

The other common challenge is a lack of context из Loose Translations Prompts that lack adequate background information may lead to outputs that are not accurate and or irrelevant. This can be avoided by providing the context that is required within the prompt. This could be background information, including data points, past data, or particular business circumstances that the AI must take into account. The prompt can be used to instruct the AI to produce more accurate and useful results by providing a rich background.

Uncertainty in requests may also cause disparity or even non-predicted results. Unclear prompts can mislead the AI, and the results can be inaccurate accordingly. In a bid to prevent this, this must be made clear. Be specific in wording and be definitive in what format you want the output to be, such as a list, a table, or a narrative. Giving such examples of what is expected and/or preferred outputs can go a long way in lending clarity to intent and expectations.

A major trap in rush-engineering is a lack of iteration and adaptation of prompts according to responses. There are continuous changes in business environments, and prompts need to be revised to meet the changes. In order to have continuous improvement, it is important to establish a feedback loop. Gathering and scrutinizing the AI results and combining user feedback can spot spots to enhance. Frequent prompts keep them good and up to date.

Testing and verification are very important to help escape traps. A proper validation process would help the outputs of the AI to be precise and meet business requirements. This may be in the form of human review, compliance checks, and iterative testing of prompts before they are provided to a business environment.

Sharing the experience of what has gone wrong with teams should help to avoid the occurrence of common pitfalls. The recording of working strategies and typical failures can be an informative background for team members. This knowledge will be shared and acted upon by the community, not only enhancing the present prompt engineering experience but also instilling an appreciation and culture of learning and adapting to the situation.

Lastly, it is important to know about the limitations of the AI models. It is important to understand when the weaknesses of a given model may impact the reliability of output and determine when people must be involved to correct the problem. Awareness of these limits will allow businesses to capitalize on AI without relying on it.

Overall, being clear about the context, iteration, validation, and sharing of knowledge can help introduce a lot of effectiveness in the prompt engineering process in avoiding the pitfalls above. In this way, AI-enabled businesses will be able to attain more precise, apposite, and effective results.

Examples of Successful Prompts

Within the business circles, productivity and specific organizational objectives have seen prompt engineering as an important tool in the promotion of productivity. The chapter explores the transformational capabilities of carefully developed prompts and, in doing so, demonstrates their usage by real-life examples that have produced measurable business success.

Consider a mid-sized e-commerce firm, which is struggling with low conversion rates at checkout. The problem facing the business was also evident; more sales should be made, without involving long-term discounting strategies that might harm the profits. By utilizing strategic prompt engineering, the company was able to create prompts that returned personalized product suggestions at every real-time customer interaction based on past browsing history and purchase intent indicators. The targeting of this campaign served not only to improve the shopping experience but also to greatly improve conversion rates, which goes to show how influential targeting is in crafting prompts in time.

In another case, the company had SaaS, and a high customer churn rate was an issue in this type of business model. Using automated prompts to analyze support tickets and usage logs, the company was able to mine the key indicators of churn that were connected with the key customer events. This information-based methodology has enabled the firm to classify its risk factors, which include integration problems and absent features, and then follow up with personalized retention offers and outreach messages. The outcome saw a significant decrease in churn rates, with customer success teams reporting on enhanced interactions with clients and hours saved in the process.

The ability of engineering to be responsive and quick is even useful in financial places where regulations may be tight. Automation through prompt-driven automation has helped a fintech company simplify its regulatory reporting functions and processes. Automating the data extraction and drafting of reports by designed prompts allowed the company to eliminate the possibility of manual errors and meet high regulatory compliance. Automation in this service saved time on report preparation, increased the accuracy and reliability of submissions, and received positive reviews among auditors.

These two examples highlight the effectiveness and multi-purpose of timely engineering in several industries. Each scenario makes a case about the role of specificity, personalization, and timing in anchoring the prompts to business goals. The key to the success of these initiatives is the possibility of converting general business problems into specific actions, which are achievable with the help of prompts that direct AI-based tools to provide clear and useful results.

The same cases indicate the possible common pitfalls, including over-automation and being mindful of brand tone, which can be eliminated with iterative refinement of prompts and their validation. The continued testing and optimization of prompts allows businesses to respond dynamically to emerging needs and keep their AI-based strategies in line with the goals of the organization.

To sum up, timely engineering application is a booster for a successful business. Maximizing processes, improving customer relations, and measurable improvement in key performance indicators are just some of the benefits that organizations can experience through the power of AI polygraphy. The latter illustrates not only the short-term gains of early engineering but also the long-term opportunities to use it as a sustainable competitive advantage in the dynamically changing business environment.

Iterative Improvement

Iterative improvement is one of the foundations of business process engineering that may be used as a tool of innovation and efficiency. As a cycle of testing, feedback, and adjustment, this process allows us to continue to refine prompts systematically so that every time around the loop, we are increasingly closer to optimal performance. The concept of iterative improvement at its core is about the ability to adopt a mindset of constant improvement, in which the individual versions of a prompt are not treated as a finished product but as a means towards a greater end: effectiveness.

The process of iterative enhancement starts with the creation of a test environment, commonly known as a sandbox, in which the new prompts can be risk-free tested with no effect on the production activity. In such an environment, experimentation can be conducted without much risk, having a place where failure is not only tolerated but forms part of the learning process. With the help of a pilot of prompts on a small group of users, the business can collect preliminary feedback and make the relevant changes prior to launching the prompts on a wider group.

The factor that is being used in iterative improvement is always carefully structured A/B testing. This can be done by developing different versions of a prompt and assigning them to different populations of users so as to compare the results. By comparing the various performances of each of these versions, companies can deduce what is working and what needs more work. Such data-based methodology makes a difference in avoiding uninformed adjustments based on a whim, but rather a prompt adjustment that is informed by empirical data.

Documentation is a central part of iterative improvement. Maintaining a traceable changelog of active versions, with a date on when they were deployed and a performance comment, helps the team track improvements along the way. Such record-keeping helps not only to have an idea of what has already been put to the test but also to obviate the recurrence of any mistakes that have been made. In addition, it allows knowledge exchange within the organization, and the teams can learn from the experiences of other people.

Safe experimentation is also important in encouraging an iterative method of improvement. Teams need to be allowed to calculate risks, knowing that not all the experiments will pay off. Such an attitude creates a culture of innovation in which mistakes are not only as essential to learn as successes. Samples of timely failures that resulted in productive lessons learned can solidify this culture based on the fact that errors are an inherent aspect of the improvement process.

The feedback loops are part and parcel of the iterative improvement cycle. Routine consultation with users and other stakeholders means that prompts are keeping abreast of the requirements of the people they aim to serve. All of this feedback should be recorded and analyzed in an effort to identify trends and areas of improvement. By enabling the users to be proactive in the process of improvement, the businesses are able to guarantee that timely advances find enough matches with the ground realities.

Last, but not least, iterative improvement is supported by continuous learning. Prompts must change to keep pace with technology and business requirements. The idea of setting up operation-continuous training and developing mechanisms means that teams will be among the leading in action, prompt engineering practice. These would entail keeping updated with the latest methods, tools, and trends relating to that field, developing or influencing cross-departmental collaboration, and sharing.

In short, iterative improvement on prompt engineering is about adopting a cycle of testing, learning, and enhancing. Therefore, by having a culture of continuous improvement, businesses are guaranteed to have their processes up-to-date and efficient in a rapidly changing environment.

CHAPTER 3

INTEGRATING PROMPT ENGINEERING INTO BUSINESS

Aligning with Business Goals

Streamlining AI capability with organizational strategy is critical to achieving business success. In fact, businesses are becoming more and more aware of the transformative power of AI in general and in the sphere of prompt engineering, in particular, which can be leveraged to drive significant business results. Implementation of swift engineering in business processes is not just a technical process but a strategic alignment process that requires a fundamental understanding of business objectives and how AI can be used to support the objectives.

The starting point in this process of alignment would be a good comprehension of core business objectives. This demands that business leaders be able to state succinctly what they want to achieve, be it operational efficiencies, deepened customer engagement, and innovation, amongst others. Now that these objectives are well articulated, what businesses can do next is to look at how exigent engineering can be done to achieve these objectives.

At the center of prompt engineering is writing accurate instructions that can lead to the creation of a particular output by an AI system. This will require close insight into the business environment as well as a clear picture of the desired results. As an example, consider that a business objective might be to increase the effectiveness of its customer support center; then, immediate engineering could be deployed to automate answers to certain common questions, thus allowing more sophisticated queries to be directed to human agents. Likewise, in dating, prompt engineering can be applied in marketing to create personalized content that appeals to the target audiences and maximizes engagement as well as conversion rates.

Besides, matching business goals with prompt engineering also needs to be done iteratively. This also includes constant testing and reformation of the prompts in order to elaborate a successful goal that they attempt to achieve. To ensure effective implementation, businesses should set up feedback loops to obtain insights on how AI-produced outputs perform and implement corrections as required. Not only can an iterative process enhance the accuracy and relevancy of the AI outputs, but it can also make sure that they remain consistent within shifting business objectives.

One more important factor of orienting prompt engineering towards business needs is to make it collaborative across divisions.

This means having mixes of multiple departmental teams, like IT, marketing, and customer service individuals, to help create and perfect prompts. With the variety of knowledge across the organization, businesses will be able to guarantee comprehensive and well-implemented AI initiatives, considering their ongoing workflow.

In addition to this, enterprises should take into account the ethical considerations of AI implementation. These include establishing guardrails to limit decisions that the AI would make that would be detrimental to the business or any of its stakeholders. It is also important to ensure the AI adheres to industry regulations and remains transparent in its operations to ensure the customers and stakeholders are assured.

Lastly, the companies ought to invest in building workforce skills and abilities in order to initiate and manage timely engineering projects successfully. This includes employee training and resource provision, where the employees will be empowered to learn and use the AI tools. By cultivating a culture of lifelong learning and innovation, companies can also ensure their AI efforts will stay in line with the overall strategies and maintain the value that they generate over time.

To summarise, however, aligning prompt engineering with business is an interactive process that necessitates tactical planning, cross-functional collaboration, and continuous refinement. Furthermore, by successfully incorporating the power of AI into their corporate strategy, companies will be able to open up brand-new vistas of expansion and sustain a high level of competitiveness in the fast-changing digital environment.

Cross-functional Collaboration

When it comes to the field of prompt engineering towards business success, it is indeed the incorporation of cross-functional collaboration that becomes really important. This not only makes the engineering to be done in a timely manner but also makes the solutions to be created holistic and objective in line with various business objectives. Multidisciplinary cooperation of different units, including the IT, HR, and Learning & Development (L&D), is critical to the integration of prompt engineering into the framework of other activities around advancing digital transformation and talent development plans.

The synergy, coupled with cross-functional collaboration, is important in overcoming the silos in an organization. Departmental isolation can cause a lack of synchronisation between the tools and approaches of various teams, as well as the overall creation of disparate targets and oversights. With cross-functional collaboration, the process of sharing know-how and resources becomes easier, leading to prompt engineering being no longer an isolated adventure but a part and parcel of company operations.

As an example, the IT departments are a key part of guaranteeing that the technological infrastructure facilitates the introduction and expansion of timely engineering solutions. Their technical skills are vital to the inclusion of new tools, platforms, and data security, as well as to inform conflicts in the work of AI systems. In the meantime, prompt engineering affords HR the opportunity to improve recruitment engagements, automate rote requests, and create training programs based on the current raft of requirements of the workforce. Prompts will enable Learning & Development teams to design individualized learning experiences that are sensitive to the level of skills current employees have, which sets the stage to grow and build skills continually.

In addition, cross-functional collaboration will motivate the creation of timely libraries, which are representative of very diverse business requirements. The ability to use knowledge gathered across departments allows these libraries to contain prompts that will result in solutions to a particular departmental issue, as well as having a part in the broader business plans. As an example, customer-support prompts can be co-created by involving the customer service team and product development teams to support an interaction that is both sensitive to customer needs and congruent with product capabilities.

Some structured feedback loops further enhance this collaborative prompt design process. Forum-like activities like brainstorming workshops, hackathons, or prompt jams are opportunities that have diverse teams work together and share their ideas and co-create solutions. Not only does it produce innovative prompts during these sessions, but it also helps develop a sense of ownership and accountability among team members because of the direct effect their input has on the outcome of the business.

Organizations can set up systems of feedback and continuous improvement that will allow continuous collaboration to take place. This incorporates instituting review meetings, providing a platform to share the obtained successes and difficulties, and rewarding contributions that have a major impact on promoting prompt performance. The practices reduce the likelihood of slow engineering practices by keeping prompt engineering dynamic and responsive to the fluctuating needs of the business environment.

In summary, a key element of effective prompt engineering is the overall cross-functional teamwork. With the ability to take advantage of the wide range of expertise within an organization, businesses can develop flexible, robust, and scalable solutions to promote business efficiency, innovation, and the ability to attain strategic alignment at all levels of an organization.

Adapting to Change

In business, change is an ever-evolving environment, and any company can ill afford to be too slow in adapting to change. Companies are currently in an era where technological changes and changes in the market are extremely high-paced. This climate forces companies of all sizes to be nimble and quick-moving to stay relevant. The practice of prompt engineering is at the core of such agility, as it provides a systematic way to utilise AI capabilities in a way that suits the changing business requirements.

This is because prompt engineering is reshaping business solutions and decision-making. With the correct prompts tailored, businesses can use AI to produce actionable, intelligent decisions to move business goals forward. This entails the disintegration of complicated business issues into smaller ones, which AI can manage well. By way of example, an organization that wants to improve customer service may break down this universal objective into more narrow action verbs, such as drafting individually crafted responses or summarizing customer interactions.

As companies maneuver in the fast-evolving operational environment, it is also important that they are ready to redesign and revise strategies on a recurrent basis. This iterative process plays a very important role in accelerated engineering, where the uptake of the first outputs of AI is unpredictable. Companies will need to be willing to go through cycles of quick refinement, where they experiment with various strategies until the desired results are realized every time. This includes modifying both the prompt itself, along with the parameters and contexts, in which they are applied. The adaptability to change the prompts based on the current feedback and outcome will keep the AI tools in tune with the changing business objectives.

Besides, the implementation of AI should be approached carefully, taking into account the compliance and ethical norms. Because more and more businesses are integrating prompt engineering into their practices, they find it essential to keep compliance with industry standards and regulations. This would involve introducing sound validation systems and the use of human-in-the-loop systems to monitor the products of the AI so that they can meet the desirable legal and ethical standards. An example is where, in regulated industries, prompts should be formulated in a way that does not produce outcomes that will cause a breach of compliance.

Along with technical adjustments, organizational culture is a significant factor in achieving change and adaptation. It is important to practice a culture that welcomes experimentation and learns in case of failures. Employees must be allowed to test new forms of prompt and even share the results with other departments to develop a culture where continuous improvement is standard. The culture of experimentation increases the productivity of rapid engineering, besides giving the employees more possibilities to contribute to the organizational agility and survival.

Last, companies should remember that they need to remain updated with changes in technology. Constant updates to AI tools, as well as the prompt libraries, are necessary in order to stay competitive. This will be characterized by keeping abreast with the current state of AI technologies and incorporating the advancements in the strategic planning of the business. By so doing, firms will be in a better position to ensure that the rapid engineering approaches they adopt are not merely knee-jerk but a proactive approach to anticipating future demands and finding themselves in the driver's seat in terms of innovation.

Overall, responding to change via timely engineering is a complex procedure that involves predictive thinking, a culture of constant upgrading, and a dedication to ethical and compliant behavior. By adopting these values, companies will be able to unlock the potential of AI to achieve success in a dynamic environment.

Measuring Success

Estimating the efficiency of prompt engineering in terms of the business environment implies the comprehensive evaluation of a number of performance indicators. These are the measures that can be used to show how effectively the integration of AI-driven prompts is addressing the business goals that were set. Both quantitative and qualitative Indicators should be taken into account so that the effects can be fully understood.

Quantitative measures are used to measure successes. These are conversion rates, time savings, cost savings, and rate of error. By way of example, an improvement in conversion rates after implementing AI prompts is an indication of the effectiveness of the prompts in encouraging customer positive responses and purchases. Similarly, the time savings possible in areas of customer support or the generation of reports can be used to exemplify the cost benefits that can lead to efficient performance in areas that involve prompt engineering. Reduction in costs, especially labour and operational costs, further brings about economic benefits associated with the use of AI prompts. Also, the error rates can be tracked before and after prompt deployment to give insights into the accuracy and reliability enhancement that automation brings.

On the qualitative level, user and stakeholder feedback can directly provide valuable input into what those using the prompts find valuable and what challenges they have to overcome. This feedback frequently consists of user feedback, ease of incorporation into the workflow, and user experience. The testimonials of the staff members who work with the prompts on a daily basis should be collected to bring out what needs to be improved and what is going well. In addition, qualitative feedback will be able to reveal unexpected positive results, such as higher morale among the employees as a result of the decreased workload or the higher level of customer satisfaction as a result of being more personable.

Businesses can keep track of success by setting up a system of measuring these metrics on a regular basis. This model normally entails the establishment of proper goals prior to the implementation of prompts that can be used as a point of comparison. By correlating the pre- and post-deployment data, companies can measure the effectiveness of timely engineering on their activity. As an example, a company wishing to decrease response time in customer support should also monitor average levels of response time before and after prompt intervention in an attempt to gauge success.

In addition, companies ought to use a continuous improvement cycle, where immediate performance is revisited and revised on a regular basis. This includes reiterative testing and correction of prompts, on the basis of performance statistics and feedback. A dynamic approach to prompt engineering will allow businesses to respond to changes and new technology changes to make sure they remain successful over time.

Also, key metrics can be presented visually using dashboards and reports that provide an effective way to get messages to stakeholders. The tools will be used to communicate the importance of timely engineering to decision-makers, which will enable them to make the best decisions strategically. By demonstrating the concrete payoff visually, businesses will be able to not only encourage their employees to recognize and support the AI initiatives within the organization but also become capable of implementing the same ones across greater levels of the organization.

To sum up, one should strike a balance between quantitative and qualitative measures of the success of prompt engineering. With an effective framework of assessment and the implementation of an organizational culture of improvement, organizations can effectively gauge success, which can lead to continued performance of AI-powered operations.

CHAPTER 4

BUILDING A PROMPT ENGINEERING TEAM

Identifying Key Skills

In the fast-paced world of the modern business, it is crucial to identify the skills that any business constantly requires to succeed. As the organizations continue to grapple with the demands and complexities of technology and market forces, being able to identify and sharpen a few skills is a strategic advantage. It is an analytical process that entails an in-depth appreciation of both present and developing capacities, and demands that businesses can remain competitive and adaptable.

Analyzing the business environment is the first approach towards identifying the key skills. This is done by reviewing the market trends in the industry, technological advancements, and competition levels. With such knowledge of these external factors, businesses can have a view of the skills that are going to be required. An example is the advent of digital change and automation, which has augmented the value of technical expertise and flexibility. Data analysis, digital literacy, and working with AI-driven tools are becoming more and more in-demand skills.

Within the company, organizations will have to evaluate their current capacity. It involves an examination of the existing workforce, what is good, and what needs to be done to help them improve. The performance reviews and skills audits are the tools that can play a significant role in this process. This would enable the organizations to map the skills they have against the identified needs so that gaps can be identified where further enhancement is necessary.

After identifying the key skills, the development strategies are the same. Continuous learning, workshops, and training sessions should be adopted to enhance skills. Enterprises have access to online platforms and in-house learning and collaborative learning environments to promote skills development. In addition, the formulation of a culture of learning and innovation can make employees develop their skills voluntarily.

The other important aspect is the correlation between the development of skills and business objectives. Skills are not to be made in a vacuum but formed as a part of forging the larger strategic goals of the organization. This convergence should mean that the development of the skills is more directly linked to business success. For example, when the company is focusing on online expansion, digital marketing, user experience design, and e-commerce skills are the primary concerns.

In addition, businesses need to have the identification of leadership in terms of skills and the development of skills. Leaders are important in all this, as they provide the vision and establish an environment that appreciates and encourages continuous learning. They are in a position to promote skill development programmes, direct resources, and offer mentorship to the process of growth.

Lastly, the performance of businesses due to learning competencies should be appraised. To assess the effectiveness of the skill development program, it is possible to use such metrics as productivity gains and innovation levels, employee engagement levels, etc. Consistent evaluation and performance improvement cycles make sure that the learning and development plan is up to date and maintains the pace with the business requirements.

Finally, key skills need to be identified as a strategic undertaking, in that an extensive knowledge of both the external and internal business environment is needed. By emphasizing skills development and linking them with business objectives, organizations can develop a workforce capable of counteracting present demands and seizing future opportunities. The active approach not only increases the performance of the business but also allows for the building of a culture of continuous improvement and innovation.

Training and Development

Training and development in prompt engineering is one of the key components that organizations that are thriving in the rapidly changing commercial environment should have in place. The introduction of artificial intelligence in business activities requires an effective system of lifelong learning and skills development, which would allow corporate teams to use the capabilities of AI-based tools as effectively as possible.

The main aspect of training and development is to have a wide-reaching, departmentalized curriculum that falls in line with the different needs of various departments and areas of expertise. This modular strategy will provide new employees, power users, and team leaders with customized content depending on the role one plays. As an example, a beginning course on prompt engineering principles can be taught during the onboarding for newcomers. In contrast, the pinpoint course can consider complex prompt crafting and optimization mechanisms taught to the experienced specialist.

This is a vital step in this learning experience, and interactive and practical activities are very important. Based on understanding business realities, the exercises give the participants the possibility to play directly with immediate, prompt engineering work, within their everyday reality. By playing games emulating real business tasks, including writing prompts to create sales email campaigns or reporting on customer complaints, the learners will practice skills learned theoretically in practice and deepen their knowledge, strengthening it by putting it into unemployment.

Organizations considering proficiency in prompt engineering can develop certification programmes. Such systems are not only an indicator of the mastery of skills but also a way to motivate ongoing learning in the form of digital badges, internal certificates, or public leaderboards. This kind of recognition creates a culture of success and growth, which motivates the employees to obtain more learning opportunities and promote the innovative potential within the organization.

Additionally, technology is changing, thus creating a need to train and upskill consistently. The trajectory of AI models and tools requires an adaptation of skills and knowledge of those operating the models in this new environment. Microlearning and quarterly refreshers will ensure that employees stay up to date with the latest developments, and peer teaching will enable the sharing of knowledge as well as the possibility of solving problems collaboratively. This lifelong upskilling makes sure that the employees are up to date with the latest trends in technology, as it allows them to implement some of the latest means of making the business a success.

Another major contribution to normalizing and scaling the practice of prompt engineering is, of course, the creation and sharing of internal prompt playbooks. The playbooks, which are organized into sections with descriptions of prompt intentions, input/output examples, use cases, and troubleshooting hints, can be valuable assets to employees. In addition to creating a reference point of best practice, this also helps to achieve consistency in timely development and use.

Promoting collaborative prompt creation is one more key to good training and development. Cross-team/departments work: Organizational culture can be shaped by holding brainstorming sessions, hackathons, cross-team/departments workshops, and other such means to instill a cultural inclination towards innovation and collective learning. Through these joint activities, the prompts are not only improved in quality, but also, many different opinions are added, which makes the solutions to the problems more holistic and successful.

To conclude, a strategic implementation of training and development in prompt engineering provides organizations with the ability to make the best use of AI tools, offering an organizational culture of permanent learning and change-embracing. Investing in systematized educational devices, rewarding good work, and inspiring teamwork boards, companies can give their staff the confidence that they can handle the demands of the approaching AI-based future.

Creating a Collaborative Environment

By establishing the conditions under which collaboration is successful, a strong emphasis should be placed on introducing mechanisms that promote inter-departmental interaction and creativity. Creating a teamworking atmosphere commences with the creation of uniform templates of departmental prompt playbooks. Such playbooks are prepared to provide a consistent and scalable approach to different teams. They contain parts describing the mission of the prompt, exemplary examples of input and output, hypothetical use cases, and advice on troubleshooting, as well as change logs. The teams are able to exercise a cohesive practice of prompt engineering using these templates, and that is invaluable to an overall cohesive effort.

Besides, the quality preparation and checking of such playbooks are essential. Appointing owners of the playbooks or rotating the writers ensures ownership and new ideas. As an example, a section on launch campaigns can be co-authored by marketing and product teams, and their expertise can be united to create efficient prompts. This not only increases the quality of the prompts but also improves the inter-departmental relations.

Easy accessibility and searchability of playbooks is also critical. One can use them by integrating them into the existing knowledge bases, wikis, or any other internal documentation platform to ensure that they are available to all team members. The ability to tag prompts by department, task, or level of compliance also makes them easier to use, as team members can view tags and easily find the information requested. Frequent updates and usage reporting, including monthly usage reports and timely performance dashboards, give insights into the applicability and relevance of such playbooks to the continuous monitoring to enhance progress.

To ease the creation of the collaborative prompt development, cross-team and cross-departmental brainstorming sessions, hackathons, or prompt jams should be held. These meetings instill an atmosphere of innovation and creativity where employees from varying departments work collaboratively in the development of new prompts. Example description: A quarterly "prompt hackathon" based on cross-functional teams of salespeople and support/operations staff can result in zero in-venue/out-of-town solutions otherwise unachievable in discrete cases.

Structured, focused feedback loops are necessary to enable quick improvement and knowledge transfer. The use of feedback forms, user surveys, and peer review will help create a continuous loop of improvements where prompts can be refined to better suit what they are being used in real-life applications and what users suggest. Awarding, rewarding, or showcasing creative or impact-driven prompt contributions through awards, publications, or some other platforms, such as Prompt of the Month, can also help to motivate employees and develop high standards.

Creating an environment where there are no failures and where experiments are encouraged is another key to building a collaborative atmosphere. The leadership messaging, role modeling, and incentives are possible to encourage iterative testing, learning after mistakes, and rapid adaptiveness. The creation of safe environments to test out new prompts and workflow, i.e., sandboxes or pilot groups, will allow employees to bite experimentation without fear of failure. Sharing and documenting the instances of the failure to act immediately and yet recovering subsequently helps in normalizing the idea of safe failure, according to which failure is considered a learning moment.

Production of a teamwork atmosphere in prompt engineering is ultimately a mixture of programmed procedures, open communication, and an encouraging culture. These strategies can be adopted in business to exploit the synergies of individual creativity and professional skills of the teams to enhance innovation and achievement in their expedited engineering services.

Leadership and Vision

In the changing environment of doing business, the role that can no longer be ignored in the process is the use of leadership to drive organizations towards success when incorporating the advanced use of technologies like prompt engineering. Leaders are challenged with the responsibility of crafting a vision that not only embraces innovation but also positions the vision within the context of the core values and strategic objectives of the organisation. This involves an understanding of technological edges as well as the overall business goals in a much-emphasized manner.

It is the first order of business that deserves a clear articulation of how these technologies can improve business processes and business outcomes by a leader in the area of prompt engineering. This means analysing particular finds where immediate engineering could provide efficiencies, brainstorming with customers, or even new value propositions. A defined, strategic focus can help leaders encourage their teams to embrace and incorporate these technologies in a manner that supports the overall business strategy.

Effective leadership here also requires a keen sense of the challenges and opportunities that accompany the adoption of AI-driven solutions. Leaders have to be active and willing to deal with issues regarding data privacy, ethical use of it, and biases that might be present in the outputs of AI. This necessitates the creation of a powerful governance infrastructure that stays in line with industry regulations and is in response to ethical principles. This not only helps the leaders to protect the organization against what might look like known risks but also earns them the trust of stakeholders and customers.

Besides, visionary leadership is associated with cultural learning and adaptation. This is essential in an industry where changes in technology are happening so fast. Leaders must inspire their teams to be up to date with what is going on in the AI field, encourage prompt engineering, and maintain a culture of experimentation and innovation. This is to be done through constant training, workshops, and joint projects that will involve employees all over the organization.

One of the most important points of leadership in the matter of prompt engineering will be the capacity to convey the advantages and consequences of these technologies to a wide audience. This is not only the technical teams but also the stakeholders who do not necessarily have a technical background. Leaders should also be able to communicate complex technical ideas that may easily be translated into simple, operational lessons that can be taken to heart by the various areas of the organization. Effective communication makes all parties realize the value of engineering in a timely manner and creates a unifying goal.

Leaders are also instrumental in incorporating urgent engineering into an organization's overall digital transformation strategies. This involves a comprehensive view that looks into how these technologies can improve current systems and processes. By synchronizing timely engineering and digital strategies, leaders can guarantee the sustainability of their organization and help it be competitive and flexible in the digital world.

When talking about leadership in a prompt engineering environment, it involves looking into the future and directing the organization towards it. It does not just imply putting in place a vision but also empowering teams to implement it with confidence and creativity. With the right leadership, an organization can use the full potential of prompt engineering to pressure the evolution of innovation, augment customer experiences, and be inclined to success in their business on a sustainable scale.

CHAPTER 5

TOOLS AND TECHNOLOGIES

Choosing the Right Tools

When it comes to the world of prompt engineering and business optimization, the choice of the tools to use is one of the essential aspects. With the growing number of businesses incorporating AI-powered technology into their workflow, the variety of available tools is rapidly growing, making the process of choosing these tools critically important and, at the same time, challenging. It is a tactical process that considers organizational interests, technicality, and the situational needs of various departments to choose the right tools.

The best way to choose the correct tools is to comprehend what business functions and objectives the AI tools serve. This includes recognizing the focus processes that may be better served using automation and expedited improvement, including customer care, marketing, human resources, and operations. By understanding how these business functions can be applied in different AI platforms, companies are able to make sure that the specific needs and prospects will be covered by the implemented tool.

Evaluation of the technical characteristics and capabilities of the tools is a vital investigation. Among the aspects that businesses should consider is how easy it would be to integrate the platform with their existing systems, how scalable a system is to support future growth, and how well the platform supports their data, security, and privacy needs based on their line of business. This means evaluating whether it meets relevant compliance requirements like GDPR or HIPAA and how easily it will be able to integrate with the CRM, marketing systems, or other enterprise software.

Another consideration is usability. The selected tools need to be workable by non-technical users, which will allow a wider pool of employees to take advantage of AI functionality without the need to develop detailed technical knowledge. This is through easy-to-use interfaces and natural language processing capabilities to correctly accept and execute commands. In addition, the tools must be flexible in the context of customization and be able to be applied across various business scenarios so that teams can customize the AI output to meet their individual brand voice and operational requirements.

Shortage is also another big factor. Companies must consider both the cost of implementing and maintaining AI tools and the possible returns and operational optimization they achieve in order to compare the costs and the benefits. This is more than just a comparison of pricing models differentiating various platforms; it also takes into account the total cost of ownership, as well as the training, maintenance, upgrade, and expansion costs.

What other businesses ought to think about is the reputation of the vendor and the type of support that is available. A secure vendor will give solid customer support, updates, and a projected path of upgrading. That will ensure that the tools can be kept relevant and effective with the way AI technologies are still changing.

Lastly, the firms must adopt a culture of trial and improvement and allow teams to test new tools and methodologies without incentive, run on a pilot basis, and later implement on a full scale. The method provides the possibility of learning and improvement in an iterative manner; this generally facilitates the maximization of the usefulness of the tools and their orientation towards business goals.

In short, the process of selecting the proper tools to use in prompt engineering is a complex one that demands great attention to be paid to business objectives, functional requirements, ease of use, affordability, and vendor support. By being smart enough to select the tools that way, businesses can optimize AI, contribute to efficiency, and attain impressive competitive advantages.

Integrating with Existing Systems

Understanding the complexities of incorporated AI tools in business systems is the precursor to integrating with current business systems, which may necessitate a sound business strategy along with technical expertise. Integration is not just a matter of fitting a new tool; it is about the integration of a new part into an already existing technology fabric of an organization. This includes the familiarization with both the features AI tools have to offer and the specifics of the existing systems they are being used on.

The initial process to be undertaken by businesses is to carry out an extensive evaluation of their existing systems. This will entail defining the main software and platforms that have been established and finding out their respective functions. The way these systems facilitate existing workflows needs to be determined by the business, and places where gaps or inefficiencies exist have to be identified as areas where AI can be used to overcome them. This preliminary analysis will become the basis of an effective integration strategy where the integration of AI improves rather than shakes up the current operations.

When the assessment is carried out, it is time to determine the appropriate AI tools that would support business interests and technical specifications. The compatibility of AI platforms with the existing systems should be considered as a part of this selection process. Compatibility must be considered since this is what defines how easily new tools will be adopted. Contemporary AI solutions also tend to have APIs (Application Programming Interfaces) and other integration features that support integrations with the existing systems and allow data flows between them.

Pilot projects are usually initiated during the integration process. Small-scale or pilot implementations give businesses a chance to experiment with the AI tools within a controlled setting, and reduce the risk of implementing an immature AI product, whilst gaining important insights on its effectiveness and outcomes. In these pilots, businesses have time to fine-tune their integration plans, ironing out any technical issues that emerge and confirming the AI tools can provide the promised rewards.

Data management can also be cited as another important aspect of integration. AI systems are data-driven, and in effective establishment, the ability to exchange information between systems in a manner that is not likely to cause a security and privacy breach is critical. This is about establishing secure data pipelines and adherence to the applicable data protection regulations. Data quality is critical as the power of AI tools largely depends on the quality of data on which they are working.

To do this, companies may use such no-code services as Zapier to automate processes in the absence of mass in-depth technological competence. These tools can be used to create workflows to automate tasks between different applications and reduce the time, effort, and custom development required in the integration process.

Besides technical considerations, change management is also needed to execute successful integration. Employees must be ready to operate with new tools and workflows; i.e., training and support are the necessary measures. This will assist in reducing resistance, coupled with a maximization of adoption, so that the integration can result in the enhancement of productivity and efficiency.

Lastly, companies need to measure the success of the integration strategies with specific metrics. These metrics need to concentrate not only on technical performance but also on business outputs, e.g., better efficiency, cost reduction, and improved decision-making. By periodically checking these metrics, businesses will be able to ensure that their AI integration is still beneficial and relevant to their strategic goals.

Staying Up-to-date

The pace of change in the world of artificial intelligence and prompt engineering is fast, and staying on top needs a pledge of lifelong learning and evolution. The industry is an evolving field and requires companies not only to keep up with technological breakthroughs but also to predict where the industry is heading further in order to embrace the power of AI to the maximum extent.

Organizations must instill a culture of keeping up with changes in AI and vigilant engineering in order to keep up with the trend. This includes the full-scale participation in a reliable online prompt library and community forums that are valuable sources of new ideas and effective practices. Such libraries may include prepackaged libraries of prompts and templates, which can be modified to suit specific business requirements and achieve overall effectiveness, while ensuring the prompts used are up-to-date and effective.

Becoming a member of industry-specific AI learning communities can substantially increase the staying-up-to-date capacity of a team. Newsletters, webinars, and discussion groups are easy ways to have constant access to the news of emerging techniques, tools, and use cases. Through this engagement, not only is knowledge development promoted, but also closeness to other members via the development of networks and pulling of peers to enhance their versatile ideas and opinions.

The practices that are important internally are to set up a clear pathway for sharing updates and making discoveries. This can be achieved with special focused communication channels, such as Slack messages or email summaries that pass on information on the latest upcoming trends and changes in the industry. Meetings or so-called AI learning hours held on a regular basis can be efficient in terms of discussing recent advancements and brainstorming on how these can be applied to streamline business processes.

The other strategic approach to the issue of staying up-to-date is the development of internal prompt playbooks. It is best to create playbooks that should be living documents in which the latest practices and learning should be incorporated. They provide a knowledge repository that can be tapped by others located in other departments within an organization, hence the consistency and scalability in its prompt application.

Furthermore, it is necessary to have a culture of experimentation that can help keep up with the changes. By keeping their risk low by providing teams with a sandbox to test new prompts and workflows, they may safely experiment and learn. This is low risk and at the same time allows teams to iterate and refine on prompts to help them achieve better results.

Innovative teams might be encouraged to explore more and more improvements and share their successful practices through recognition and celebration of their innovative prompt contributions. Rewards or internal displays of eminent prompt implementations can excite and create impetus for innovation in the organization.

Lastly, mechanisms that conduct technology and process audits on a frequent basis should also be put in place. The audits play a role in enabling the organization to ensure that its AI capabilities are kept in line with the business objectives and technological changes. Regular audits of the platforms and timely performance will help in identifying the weak spots and ways to introduce new instruments or approaches.

The practices mentioned above can be incorporated into the organizational culture of a business to not only keep up with the current prompt engineering trends but also present the business as a leader in harnessing the potential of AI as a business tool. Such a proactive orientation towards remaining current facilitates the organization being sufficiently prepared to manage future changes and remain competitive in an increasingly AI-driven environment.

Security and Compliance

Security and compliance are of the essence in the world of prompt engineering. Companies are expected to maneuver through the frequently complex environment of regulatory requirements and best practices in order to safeguard sensitive data, but use AI technologies to their advantage. It starts with the understanding of the risks that necessarily come with AI and data handling. When sensitive data levels are not managed adequately, the organization and its stakeholders may suffer because of data integrity, loss of business goodwill, and customer faith.

One of the most significant features of the security maintenance is the adherence to the strict data privacy regulations. This entails anonymizing and reducing the data that are applied in the AI prompts to avoid unauthorized access or leaks. Organisations are advised to use placeholders rather than operational data in the testing environment and to blank out sensitive data being fed into AI. Such practice not only secures sensitive data but also coincides with privacy laws, including GDPR and CCPA.

In addition, businesses are required to introduce effective workflow controls to allow the detection of any accidental disclosure. This involves designing automatic filters that can stop prompts that include confidential words and approval procedures for prompts that are in regulated sectors. With such policies, firms will be in a position to limit the number of people who can access sensitive prompts, which in turn decreases the possibility of illicit exposure of sensitive information.

Another cornerstone of secure prompt engineering is compliance. Organizations need to acquaint themselves with important regulatory laws such as GDPR, HIPAA, and CCPA that address data protection and privacy. Customized compliance checklists for particular industries will help achieve these rules. As an example, in the healthcare industry, healthcare-related prompts must be phrased in a way that no personal health information (PHI) is revealed, whereas, in financial processing, financial industry prompts must not publish or non-approved forward-looking statements.

One of the keys to regulatory alignment is integrating compliance procedures into everyday tasks. This will include insisting on pre-deployment compliance reviews of new or revised prompts and the standardization of complete documentation. This documentation should describe who reviewed the prompt, when it was reviewed, and what was approved, and it will provide an audit trail to further accountability and transparency.

Outside of compliance, ethical considerations must be followed in the implementation of AI. Companies are advised to have a business AI ethics policy that draws on working and societal values in order to support the use of responsible AI. This involves undertaking risk assessment to determine the possible ethical problems and establishing incident reporting and rapid action plans in the event that some problems occur after deployment.

Lastly, organizations are supposed to adopt a learning and adaptation culture in security and compliance practice. Having regular privacy trainings and appointment of data stewards will be of great help in keeping the standard of data protection high. Moreover, being aware of the constant upgrades and industry standards tenets helps companies to be compliant and safe in their dealing with AI.

Rather than focusing on security and compliance, companies can show customers and stakeholders that they care about security, ensuring that not only is their data safe, but customers can also develop confidence in their services. This is the promise of preserving the information and meeting the demands that will allow firms to utilize AI technologies to their full potential and reduce the risks of data breach and non-compliance.

CHAPTER 6

DEVELOPING PROMPT LIBRARIES

Creating Standardized Templates

In the world of prompt engineering, creating a core of standardized templates is an important prerequisite to the consistency and scalability of business operations. The formulation of these templates entails a careful process so that they can be relied upon as templates to provide precise and effective results to the AI systems.

This is initiated by defining the central elements that the templates are to encompass. This incorporates specifying the intent of the prompt, that is, the carrying cushion of the intended use. With the defined objective, the prompt can be customized to attend to particular business requirements, such as customer support, marketing, or operations. This interpretability avoids ambiguity and lets the AI system know what is wanted.

Moreover, the standardized templates should contain sample input and outputs as well. These examples are to serve as benchmarks that the AI can use to determine whether its responses are appropriate. Demonstrating such examples can help define performance expectations as well as train the AI to harmonize with the requirements and objectives of the company.

Another important step is the incorporation of the use case into the templates. Examples of applications of the prompts to different business scenarios allow companies to picture the real-life implementation of the templates in different business sectors. With this step, a greater insight into how efficient and productive prompt engineering is can be realized in real-life situations.

Standardized templates also include troubleshooting sections. Such sections provide resolutions and advice in solving general problems that may occur when implementing prompts. When possible challenges are pre-emptively tackled, businesses can be in a better position to streamline their operations as well as minimize downtime due to unexpected issues.

Besides, it is important to have updated logs in the templates to keep track of revisions and enhancements. This practice is important in that all the involved stakeholders are informed about the changes and are in a position to adopt new strategies or tools when they change. It also supports a culture of constant improvement, in which feedback and performance analytics are applied to optimise and improve the effectiveness of prompts.

To create these templates, the process must be collaborative, where cross-departmental employees bring different perspectives and ideas. Having certain people/groups with ownership of templates promotes responsibility and will support frequent changes and reviews. Rotating contributors are also able to bring new opinions to the table, and this is because they might result in stagnation and innovation.

These templates must be inserted into the knowledge management systems of the organization, e.g., in a wiki or internal documentation system, to maximize access and utility. In this way, they can be conveniently searched and accessed by any employee, thus establishing a common practice of timely engineering.

The designing of standardized templates remains neither a generic process nor the final; it is an ongoing process of iterative refinement and adjustment. Prompts that drive AI interactions have to change as technology and business requirements change. By creating a framework of template creation and maintenance that is robust in nature, the business can unlock the power that lies in AI, utilizing consistency, precision, and innovation as the key to success.

Ensuring Consistency and Quality

In prompt engineering, the challenges of consistency and quality should be the major tasks, with enough attention to detail. The flexibility of AI application outputs requires a well-established structure of validation and review to ensure the outcome is in line with pre-set business objectives and expectations. Closure to this process will be the step of constructing clear prompts that avoid ambiguity. Defining action words and particular results would go a long way in ensuring that the output of the responses put in by the artificial intelligence has decreased variability, and therefore, a better output stream.

A major element in this process is the formulation of a validation workflow, which involves human supervision. This makes AI results not only correct, but also relevant and in conformance with all the required regulations and internal guidelines. The process usually follows a series of steps where humans can review AI-created content to ensure it meets the business requirements: accuracy, relevance, and the ability to pass business, legal, and brand compliance. This is necessary to ensure that there will be no compliance problems since some industries may be heavily regulated.

In addition, AI outputs are also made consistently by the use of internal prompt libraries. Such libraries are repositories of standardized prompts that can be reused by multiple departments and tasks, thus allowing all the teams to have the same playbook. With frequent improvement and evaluation of such libraries, companies will be able to keep the quality of AI output high. This further leads to scalability, meaning that the quick engineering practices can be easily borrowed and varied across the various teams or departments of an organization.

The use of guardrails is also one of the adopted strategies that helps maintain quality and uniformity. These guardrails are control parameters within the prompts that confine the AI's output to set boundaries and mitigate against off-brand or dangerous action. As an example, prompts may be trained to avoid specific response types or to use the exact brand voice/tone of the company. This is more so in applications where the company deals directly with customers whose perception of any slightest deviation from the brand standard could have a negative impact on its reputation.

Besides all this, continued training and upskilling of personnel tasked with responding to timely engineering is essential. Periodical workshops and training may keep the working community abreast with the current best practices and technological innovations. This learning culture is ongoing and makes team members feel free to experiment and continuously refine the prompts, and therefore enhances the overall AI outputs.

Lastly, feedback loops are also an important element in achieving continuous improvement in prompt engineering. By regularly gathering and interpreting the feedback of AI users, companies will be able to determine patterns and improvement areas of their prompts. The iterative cycle of refinement not only improves the quality of outputs but also makes outputs more business-aligned, too, since it is driven by feedback in the real world.

Finally, to establish consistency and quality in timely engineering, one should devise various solutions, including accurate crafting of the prompt, human supervision, standard libraries, guardrails, training, and feedback utilities. By coupling these aspects with their AI plans, companies can work the magic of AI without jeopardizing the standards required to make a business flourish.

Updating and Maintaining Libraries

In the ever-changing environment in which business is conducted, it has become very important to ensure that libraries are kept current and in good shape. One way to achieve prompt engineering is by using a viable tool that can lead to business excellence and ensure that these libraries are current and properly maintained. Among the key elements of the process is getting a solid system of updating libraries and maintaining libraries with templates of prompt responses and frameworks. Such a platform has to be dynamic and can integrate new knowledge and changing business demands.

The initial thing in this process is the development of a methodical arrangement that will carry regular reviews and updates. This includes initiating regular review of the prompt libraries so that they are in tandem with the prevailing business goals and technology changes. These reviews must be made quarterly, and teams will be able to reflect on the performance of the existing prompts and areas of improvement. This way, businesses can always make sure that their prompt libraries are continually in line with the newest trends and practices within the industry.

Beyond scheduled reviews, library ramifications can best be done through a feedback loop. This will entail receiving feedback from various users in various departments to ascertain the level of functioning of the prompts used in realistic situations. Feedback may be obtained based on surveys, interviews with the user, or direct observation of their use of prompts in everyday activities. By collecting this feedback, businesses will be in a position to know which prompts require improvement or replacements, thereby keeping the library as a worthwhile resource.

Another essential item in keeping of timely libraries is version control. Tracking variations of prompts effectively provides the opportunity to rollback if a new variant does not work as anticipated. Also helps in learning how prompts have evolved through time and gives you useful insights about what modifications proved effective. It will be necessary to implement a clear version control system that will keep detailed logs of the changes and updates made to the prompt library to ensure its integrity and reliability.

However, more than internal updates, it is important to keep abreast of external developments in technology and industry standards. Businesses must follow the corresponding newsletter, be members of professional discussion groups, and attend webinars in order to remain informed about the latest advances in AI and timely engineering. This outside contribution can offer new visions and thoughts that can be merged into the established library so it can keep pace with the world's developments.

In addition, businesses must develop a list of best practices to update and keep libraries. This involves recommendations that can accompany quick creation, e.g., Clarity, brevity, and enabling business objectives. This should also be emphasized to ensure that legal and ethical requirements are met in all prompts, especially regarding the privacy and security of data. A set of best practices documented centrally can be used to provide consistency and quality in the prompt library.

Lastly, making continuous improvement and innovation a culture is essential in the long run for maintaining prompt libraries. Allowing teams to experiment with new ideas and prompts and be willing to share their failures and successes can result in important discoveries and innovations. Appreciating and celebrating the extent of contributions to the library will also encourage teams to participate in the maintenance process.

In recap, the maintenance and updating of libraries is a constant process that must be planned strategically, reviewed on a regular basis, supported by active feedback mechanisms, and committed to constant development. It is in the following of these principles that businesses may rest assured that their prompt libraries continue to be an effective factor in contributing to their success in ever-changing business environments.

Sharing Across the Organization

The integration of timely engineering in the operations of a business involves strategic considerations that are aimed at ensuring that knowledge is properly developed and shared with other persons within the business. This entails designing in-house playbooks, which are comprehensive solution tools that can be used immediately to assist different departments in taking advantage of AI tools. These playbooks are supposed to be standardized and share a common template so as to make them uniform and easy to read. The most important parts may consist of the goal of prompts, examples of input and output, application scenarios, fixes, and a changelog. This kind of an organized plan ensures that every member of the team is well aware of what prompt engineering practice includes, and is able to incorporate prompt engineering efficiently, even when they are not much into the technical part of it.

In order to create a culture of collaboration, continuous improvement, and multi-authorship, it would be necessary to introduce mechanisms to co-author and review these playbooks. By having ownership of specific material assigned to people or teams and rotating contributors, the resource can remain dynamic with up-to-date information or other materials. As an example, the marketing and product teams could co-write on topics to use during launch campaigns to make sure the prompts are useful in implementation. Also, some methods should be established to make these playbooks accessible and searchable in the organization. This can be implemented through integration with existing knowledge bases, wikis, or any internal documentation platform that will enable any employee to easily find what they are looking for based on department, task, or level of compliance.

Semi-frequent reports and analytics are key to monitoring the reach and the effectiveness of prompt engineering throughout the company. Monthly usage reports, dashboards of key performance indicators, and feedback forms can be a good source for understanding how prompts are used and what is required to improve them. A leaderboard of the most-used prompts on the company intranet can also facilitate engagement and innovation.

The cross-team/departmental rapid development sessions can be organized as well to increase the levels of cooperation and innovation. Brainstorming sessions, hackery exercises, or prompt jams that involve cross-functional teams of sales, support, and operations people can be a way to start coming up with better prompts. Structured feedback loops are also essential for timely repair and knowledge transfer. These may be in the form of feedback forms, user surveys, and peer reviews, and initiatives such as "Prompt Review of the Month," which encourages suggestions and improvements to be made anonymously.

Best practices with regard to capturing, codifying, and acting on feedback must be defined. This incorporates keeping revisions, records, and open revision policies to ensure that all the feedback is recorded and carried out deliberately. Awarding and acknowledging innovative or high-impact prompt contributions in a newsletter, showcase, or elsewhere can also encourage employees to be constructively involved in prompt engineering.

Altogether, the dissemination of prompt engineering knowledge within an organization requires a well-structured framework to ensure the generation, sharing, updating, and advancement of prompts within an organization. By establishing a team approach and leveraging the use of organized resources and feedback systems, companies will be able to make timely engineering an embedded element of their professional strategy, instilling efficiency and a diversity of innovation organizational-wide.

CHAPTER 7

CASE STUDIES OF SUCCESS

Retail and E-commerce

Customer engagement/sales conversion is the element that companies are always trying to optimize in the ever-changing environment of retail and e-commerce. Leveraging such advanced AI technologies as prompt engineering has transformed the way retailers deal with consumers and how they run their businesses. The core capability behind this transformation is the potential to personalise interactions and suggestions dependent on specific customer requirements and enhance the overall buying experience, thus leading to increased sales.

The major challenge that most retailers face is the low conversion rate at the checkout stage, which is considered to be one of the most important stages where potential sales are usually lost. The common problem is abandoned carts, which leads to a high loss of revenue. Retailers have tapped prompt engineering as a way of resolving this challenge to provide personalized shopping journeys. By using information on what customers have searched for and their purchase goals, individualized reminders can be created to remind them of something very similar to what they are in need of or what they desire. This real-time personalization will motivate customers to make their purchases, increasing their level of conversions.

It starts with customer data analysis in searching patterns and preferences. The specified data-based practice provides the opportunity to generate the prompts that are both current and relevant, which increases the chance of their engagement. An example of this would be that when a customer spends a lot of time on a certain set of goods, recommendations can be made to relate to or offer accompanying goods, thereby increasing the facade of a purchasing experience.

In addition, A/B testing is also used to streamline these prompts. Creating various messaging strategies and formats will allow retailers to figure out which prompts lead to the most conversions. Such a reiterative process is useful to make the prompts more dynamic and reactive to the changing consumer behavior and preferences.

The effect of implementing prompt engineering is not limited to the checkout process. It is also a major contributor to customer retention as well as customer loyalty. One of the ways to engage customers on a continuing basis is to personalize the follow-up messages or send exclusive offers via prompts. This continuous communication not only leads to loyalty but also adds to a series of repeat purchases, which play key roles in long-term business success.

The specificity and personalization of the prompts might be considered one of the most important characteristics of prompt engineering that make it successful in retail. Instead of generalizing, prompts will be created to reflect a specific customer need and preference. This level of accuracy promotes the timeliness of the communication process, and customers will feel important and listened to.

Nonetheless, there are also some problems related to the promotion of prompt engineering. Too much automation and a lackluster tone can negatively affect the quality of prompts, causing them to fail to engage recipients and ultimately convert instead. Thus, retailers should strike a balance between automation and the human factor, and the prompts should have the voice and message of the brand.

Overall, the combination of prompt engineering with retail and e-commerce has made it possible to give a business a strong tool for creating customer involvement and converting it into a business. Personalizing customer interaction and utilizing customer data allows retailers to increase conversions and establish long-term customer relationships. With the ongoing changes in retail environments, prompt engineering will remain an essential element of effective e-commerce programs and help the company to stay competitive in a fast-changing retail world.

Finance and Banking

In the finance and banking sector, the realization and adoption of AI-enabled prompt engineering have brought in a paradigm shift. This new technology is transforming long-established processes through increasing practicality, precision, and consumer convenience. Prompt engineering may become the most significant tool as financial institutions face the problem of excess volumes of data being processed daily and have to find a way to simplify the work and enhance their decision-making processes.

Automation of routine tasks is another one of the main spheres in which rapid design is bringing great changes. Banking professionals and financial analysts tend to deal with repetitive tasks that include data entry, financial transaction processing, and report composition. With the use of AI-based prompts, these tasks can be automated, liberating time that the professionals can utilize in more strategic undertakings. Not only does such a move increase productivity, but it also reduces the risk of human error, which plays a major role in an industry where accuracy is key.

Furthermore, the innovative engineering helps to deliver a powerful set of customer care solutions with the help of smart chatbots and virtual assistants. The AI-powered tools can effectively manage a broad span of customer requests, such as balances, transactions, and more, in real-time. With correct prompt responses, the banks can enhance the satisfaction and loyalty of a large number of customers. These tools may also be programmed so that they can escalate certain complex issues to human agents, giving customers the best possible attention.

Prompt engineering is of benefit to risk management, which is one of the fundamental aspects of the financial sector. With the help of IA, one can review massive amounts of information to detect trends and irregularities that may reflect possible threats, including fraud or credit defaults. With the help of carefully constructed prompts, financial institutions are able to raise alarms and reports before these dangers materialize, protecting their assets and staying regulation-compliant. This aggressive behavior not only safeguards the institution but also builds confidence in the stakeholders and the clients.

In this case, prompt engineering is very useful for compliance and regulatory reports. The financial industry is highly regulated, and close attention to compliance regulations is an absolute must. The prompts provided by AI can be used to automate the production of reports compliant with these standards, so no information required is left unreported and presented late. Not only does this ease the workload of compliance teams, but it also does so in a manner that decreases the financial loss of non-compliance penalties.

Moreover, engineering of prompt-based financial forecasting and analysis is gaining currency in terms of its strategic use. Financial institutions can analyse historical information and gain insights into trends by using AI to uncover more accurate forecasts and models. Such knowledge can be used to make more strategic planning and investment choices and create an edge for the institution in the competitive market down the road.

The adoption of prompt engineering in the finance and banking industry does not come without challenges. Institutions need to consider data privacy and data security and make sure that their sensitive financial data is secured according to regulatory requirements, such as GDPR. Also, the constant monitoring and optimization of AI models are necessary to ensure their effectiveness and applied relevance in a fast-developing financial situation.

In sum, prompt engineering is transforming the sphere of finance and banking as it can increase work efficiency, improve the relationship with customers, and enrich the risk system. As financial institutions consider the usage of these technologies, they situate themselves in the leading positions in terms of innovations, ready to quickly overcome the emerging complexity of the modern financial world.

Healthcare and Pharmaceuticals

Application of AI-driven prompt engineering in the field of healthcare and pharmaceuticals is experiencing considerable forward steps. This has started to reform traditional practices, spur efficiency, and result in improved patient outcomes. The healthcare field has long had its perks in the precision and flexibility of AI technologies.

Prompt engineering in healthcare is the practice of developing custom guidance to tell the AI systems how to derive actionable intelligence from huge datasets. Applications: This is an important step in medical diagnostics, where AI may be used to process the complicated data recorded about patients, imaging data, and genetic data. AI systems can recognize patterns and outliers that may not be seen by a human eye via their use of exactly designed prompts, therefore allowing prompt intervention.

Also, in the pharmaceutical industry, AI is being used in drug discovery and development. The discovery process of a new drug is usually tedious and expensive. However, using AI, researchers can emulate thousands of chemical reactions and forecast possible drug candidates at an order of magnitude faster and less expensively. Prompt engineering is critical in this scenario since it allows for the development of queries that will help an AI system navigate a very large chemical space productively.

In healthcare facilities, AI-powered prompts are applied to improve the efficiency of administrative tasks, and thus, more time is dedicated to the treatment of patients. As an example, scheduling, billing, and patient record management can be automated with the use of AI systems. When designed with intelligent prompts, these systems can help make sure that information falls into the right categories and can be easily located, helping mitigate administrative demands and minimizing the risks of error.

The other topic in which prompt engineering is proving helpful is patient engagement. Chatbots programmed with particular prompts can communicate with patients, give information, remind them about medication times, and even give preliminary assessments, depending on the symptoms that the patients describe. This has the benefit of enhancing patient compliance with treatment regimes as well as empowering the patient since they have access to adequate and relevant information and support at the right time.

Moreover, within the sphere of personalized medicine, immediate or real-time engineering will allow optimizing the treatment regimen according to specific data about a patient. By asking specific questions, it is possible to use AI tools to provide a genetic profile, lifestyle factors, and medical history as the basis to recommend a unique treatment option. This case-by-case application not only increases the efficacy of treatment but also reduces the adverse effects, thereby resulting in better patient outcomes.

Nevertheless, there are some challenges associated with the integration of AI in the health care and pharmaceutical sectors. In this case, the key aspects will be data privacy and compliance with regulations like HIPAA. An elaborate protocol should be entrenched in prompt engineering to protect patient data and ensure the AI results are within the legal framework and meet ethical requirements. This is done by establishing strong guardrails and validation procedures to analyse the AI-generated insights, prior to these findings being put into clinical or pharmaceutical use.

On the whole, this reflective ability in the context of prompt engineering within the healthcare and pharmaceutical industries is a testament to the revolutionary capabilities of AI. As a result of better diagnostics and faster drug development, patient engagement, and overall improvement of the healthcare system, prominent engineering is opening the door to a new and more efficient healthcare system. With the ongoing technological growth, it is possible to expect even greater potential of AI in both these areas, which can drive further changes and advancement in the sphere of treating patients.

Technology and Startups

With the rapidly changing world of technology, startups become the pioneers of innovation, harnessing the latest tools to change traditional business models radically. These young firms are the best placed to bank on the innovations in artificial intelligence and machine learning, especially by strategically implementing prompt engineering. This new field is not simply an expert talent but a life-changing method of empowering new businesses to streamline operations, improve customer relations, and increase performance.

Startups are also formally nimble, able to absorb new technology quickly; this is quite essential in the competitive technology market. Such companies are flexible in incorporating solutions that are driven by AI, which will enable them to test the various applications of prompt engineering. When creating specific and contextually aware prompts, startups will be able to make sure that the results provided by the AI system are relevant to the targeted business goals. This accuracy is critical in activities like automating customer care, personalizing marketing functions, and simplifying product development.

The process of fitting the prompt engineering into startup activities requires starting by identifying the fundamental business problems that can be resolved using AI. Most startups are resource-limited, so time efficiency is a key consideration. Through prompt engineering, they have the option of automating mindless procedures, which releases human resources to engage in more strategic operations. As a case in point, not only can AI be used to respond to customer requests, compose e-mails, or provide data-based analytics, but AI also saves a significant amount of time and effort on the part of human teams.

Besides, startups can take advantage of prompt engineering to improve their products. With the help of AI to access market trends and customer feedback, startups can also optimize their products and services to satisfy the customers. This would be especially helpful in sectors of the economy like e-commerce, where insights on consumer behavior could translate to more focused advertising and user experience.

One more benefit that startups experience due to the immediate configurations of engineering is the capacity to fail fast. The startup environment is highly dynamic, and this means that a fast rate of change is critical in ensuring the replacement and modification of short-term business strategies. Prompt engineering ensures the necessary instruments for the startups so that they can test different situations and results and proceed in decision-making, basing it on AI-generated information. This cyclic procedure not only reduces the pace of product production but also increases responsiveness to the market, which provides startups with a competitive advantage.

Additionally, startups commonly have a niche market where a relationship is a key element in terms of customer experiences. Prompt engineering makes it easy to create tailored interactions so that communications will be relevant and interesting. By utilizing the power of AI to handle a large stream of data, startups will be able to narrow down their audience and present highly customized content that will appeal to a specific customer.

Lastly, the scalability of prompt engineering makes it a good solution that is suitable for startups that are set to advance. This is because the bigger these companies grow, the more pressing the need to implement scalable solutions, but that will also continue to journey towards quality and efficiency. The engineering offered by a company like Prompt Engineering can scale up with it, and this means that the processes driven by AI can still stay up to the requirements of an expanding customer list.

In summary, the synergy between technology and startups is described perfectly through the utilization of timely engineering. All these not only make the company more efficient but also stimulate innovation and customer satisfaction. Embarking on an AI journey means being able to develop the entire AI cycle internally and ensuring its success by incorporating prompt engineering into the core strategies. This way, startups can use the full potential of AI and become leaders in the industries.

CHAPTER 8

ETHICS AND COMPLIANCE

Understanding Ethical Considerations

Ethical considerations are an important aspect of practice in the field of prompt engineering because they are critical in making sure that artificial intelligence tools are used ethically. The adoption of AIs into business processes has raised concern about the need for ethical guidelines to govern the utilitarian application of such technologies as they continue to take a front seat in business processes across different industries.

The bias issue is one of the bases of ethics in AI. One important thing to note is that AI systems may hold on to or even deepen biases already present in the data that they are being trained on. This is even more worrying in aspects like employment or policing, where prejudiced algorithms may result in the unfair treatment of certain groups of people. As such, companies need to deploy stringent mechanisms that counter bias in the AI-generated outputs. This involves carrying out frequent audits and including different teams in the development process to present a different point of view that might assist in detecting any bias that may be present.

Another serious ethical issue is transparency. Stakeholders and users must be aware of the way AI systems make decisions. They will have to document and convey how requests are framed and the information that will be used. Transparency fosters trust and allows accountability since it provides a platform to comprehend and question AI-driven decisions. Businesses must endeavor to make their AI processes as transparent as possible, with the end-user having the ability to access explanations regarding the manner in which results are produced.

Privacy is also an ethical concern of great significance to prompt engineering. IT systems could be the biggest consumers of data in order to be efficient, and there is an issue of data collection, storage, and use. Companies are required to comply with data protection laws, e.g., GDPR, and have a solid data governance system that protects users' information. These include limiting the amount of data collected to the bare minimum and anonymizing data wherever necessary.

Also, accountability of the AI systems is essential. Since AI systems perform tasks that were previously the role of humans, it becomes complicated to establish responsibilities in decisions made by AI systems. Businesses should develop effective accountability mechanisms that would ensure there is a human to monitor AI-enabled systems and make necessary decisions. Such human scrutiny is important in keeping the standards of ethics and carrying out investigations of the problems that may occur due to outputs of AI.

Finally, corporations should look at the future of society, which will be affected by AI technologies. Although AI can increase efficiency and advance innovation, it is also likely to cause the loss of jobs and create a difference between those who can access technology and those who cannot. Businesses are urged to include themselves in the debate to understand the wider impact of AI and find solutions that will ensure inclusivity and fair access to technology.

To conclude, the identification of ethical considerations in prompt engineering and their consideration is a vital part of practical AI deployment. Giving attention to bias mitigation, transparency, privacy, accountability, and societal influence, businesses will be able to make sure their AI systems are not only successful but ethical and adherent to the interests of the greater society. This method is not only low risk but also makes AI more capable of making a positive impact on business efficiency and the development of society in general.

Implementing Compliance Measures

Comprehensive integration of compliance measures into business operations is critical in keeping the business compliant and with no risk to the brand. This is a complex process consisting of three interacting areas: regulatory awareness, planning, and careful implementation.

The initial hurdle to the compliance process is familiarity with the regulatory laws relevant to your particular industry. GDPR data privacy compliance. GDPR is not alone on the list of regulatory compliance, as HIPAA and CCPA follow suit in data protection. This will include not only acquainting oneself with the contents of the legislation, but also translating said requirements into steps within the business operational framework.

This can be done through the realization of practical compliance checklists that are specific to the industries. These checklists can be followed as points of reference to make sure that they do not overlook any of the compliance requirements during the prompt engineering process. In healthcare, prompts need to be written in a way that personal health information (PHI) is omitted and that they follow HIPAA requirements. On the same hand, financial services should not make unauthorized predictions that could land the business in trouble with financial regulations.

Another important element is the ability to embed compliance checks into the day-to-day workflows. This may be realized through the need to undergo pre-deployment reviews of new or adjustments to the prompts. Development of an accelerated approval matrix, as well as the definition of the roles of reviewers, will make it possible for all prompts to be reviewed against compliance before being implemented. This matrix also performs a protective function since it clearly documents who checked and approved each prompt, thus producing an audit trail that can be used as needed.

Further, it is imperative to have current documentation on compliance and audit trails. This will entail establishing a standard of documentation that will indicate the persons reviewing the prompts, the date of review, and what was approved. These records not only help show compliance but also allow audits to run more smoothly and provide a documented history of compliance adherence.

Businesses are advised to establish review cadences so that compliance is maintained continuously. This may include a quarterly review of compliance measures, where compliance and legal teams would determine the effectiveness of the measures in place and make adjustments. This is adaptive and enables businesses to be ahead of regulatory amendments, thereby making business compliance a strong and successful strategy.

In addition to these internal measures, businesses might also consider external audits or reviews by third-party experts. Such audits can provide an unbiased assessment of compliance practices and highlight areas for improvement. By inviting external perspectives, companies can gain insights that might be overlooked internally, thereby enhancing their compliance strategies.

Implementing compliance measures is not just about avoiding fines or penalties. It is about fostering trust with customers, partners, and stakeholders. By demonstrating a commitment to compliance, businesses can enhance their reputation, build stronger relationships, and ultimately achieve greater success in their operations. This approach not only mitigates risk but also positions the company as a leader in ethical business practices, which can be a significant competitive advantage in today's market.

Balancing Innovation and Regulation

The tension between innovation and regulation is crucial in the changing world of business, where regulation is required to balance the overall effect created. In the rush to leverage AI and timely engineering, companies must understand the nuance of their industrial regulatory landscape. This twofold focus necessitates a strategic direction that would embrace the opportunities of new technologies and safeguard the laws and regulations that are currently in place.

At the core of this balance, there must be a strong structure that combines innovative products and complies with the regulations. The first step that businesses ought to undertake is to familiarise themselves with the regulatory environment that is relevant to their practice. This entails extensive due diligence on all the existing laws and guidelines that can affect the implementation of AI technologies. Major regulatory acts like GDPR, HIPAA, and CCPA, among others, in turn, serve as the pillars of compliance and determine the data management, sharing, and protection.

Instead, innovation requires a progressive mindset that welcomes experimentation and change. Organizations are expected to develop a culture where innovation in finding solutions is no longer a one-off initiative but a systematic part of business strategy. This includes the creation of sandbox environments, whereby new ideas can be field-tested without risk of non-compliance. The controlled environments enable the consideration of new solutions and guarantee the possibility of ensuring regulatory violations are discovered and resolved at the early stages.

Furthermore, the importance of human control in achieving a balance between these two forces cannot be overestimated. Human-in-the-loop procedures are also essential gateways in the AI implementation process, in which appropriate outputs warrant compliance with both corporate and legal standards. These processes require human input at some crucial steps, like the reviews of AI-generated text as far as compliance and relevance are concerned. Through the human oversight of businesses, risks that are related to AI, including bias and inaccuracies, can be minimized, increasing the trustworthiness and reliability of the AI systems that businesses utilize.

The placement of a guardrail also helps keep this balance, as it is a strategic implementation. Guardrails are predefined constraints on the premises on which AI systems can operate, eliminating the possibility of output causing regulatory breaches. These are limitations to data use, generation of content, and formats of outputs, and are all designed to fit a certain guideline to regulations. These guardrails allow companies to embed regulatory protections in AI practices that will help avoid compliance violations and protect their reputation.

Also, ongoing training and education of workers on innovation and regulation are important. This will help ensure that the teams are not only conversant with the most recent technology updates but also with the regulatory aspects of what they are engaged in. Ad-hoc training and periodic workshops should enable employees to innovate within the limits of compliance and develop a healthy culture of responsible innovation.

Lastly, it is required to cooperate with different departments in areas such as legal, compliance, and IT. Such a process of collaboration enables consideration of all the various aspects of innovation and regulation. It ensures decisions are made with full knowledge of the full scope of their consequences. Through collaboration, these units are able to come up with more comprehensive strategies that deliver innovation but within compliance parameters, allowing a symbiotic balance to be reached between the two.

In sum, the question of innovation and regulation is a matter of balance that demands ongoing monitoring, flexibility, and cooperation. By building a strong framework combining these factors, companies will be able to navigate turbulent regulatory waters whilst making use of the opportunities that technology has made available. This balance can not only ensure regulatory compliance by protecting it but also places businesses at the head of innovative industrial and commercial solutions that enable techno-economic sustainability.

Case Studies in Ethical Prompt Engineering

The environment of early design is as colorful as it is transformative, and moral concerns represent a very important aspect of early design implementation. Investigating real-life use cases offers a more in-depth look at how the potential of ethical prompt engineering can be used to make businesses successful and still operate within ethical and legal boundaries of compliance and trust.

Think of a medium-sized e-commerce company that struggles with checkout conversions. The company has implemented AI prompts to personalize customer interaction and generate real-time products based on browsing history and purchase intent. Such a strategy not only increased conversion rates but also demonstrated the positive use of AI as it managed to honour the privacy and preferences of customers, meaning that the recommendations were relevant yet non-obtrusive.

In a second case, a SaaS business was experiencing an excessive turnover. Since they would look at support tickets and use logs in real-time as they used the prompt engineering, they could see churn signs. This data-modelling strategy enabled the company to develop individualised retention offers that sharply decreased the rates of churn, proving that timely engineering can make ethical gains on customer retention practices without resorting to manipulative practices.

A fintech firm, which had to cope with highly complicated compliance reporting, explored prompt engineering to automate the extraction of data as well as the drafting of the reports. The use of AI-generated prompts optimized the compliance journey and minimized human error as each prompt was regulated to maintain terminology and formatting. This case highlights the essence of ethical vigilance engineering in ensuring compliance with the regulations and reducing human error, which can prove expensive in terms of economic and image costs.

In the field of consulting, companies have been able to utilize prompt engineering to speed up market research and competitive analysis and thus minimize the time spent on manual research. Integrating prompts to build a smooth workflow of ingesting data, analysis, and report issuance has enhanced client satisfaction and shortened the turnaround time. As this case shows, ethical prompt engineering can be an efficient driver without compromising the integrity of the research process.

Finally, a big company with a difficult challenge of screening a huge number of resumes needed during the massive hiring experience prompted engineering capability to automate rankings of the candidates, as well as the extraction of skills. By incorporating the outputs of AI mechanisms into their human review practices, they both increased recruitment efficiency and mitigated the level of bias, providing a just and fair recruitment mechanism. This underlines the possibility of ethically engineering promptness to foster diversity and inclusion practices in human resources.

These case studies explain how ethical prompt engineering plays a central role in different business situations. They show that an engineering approach towards privacy, compliance, and fairness can enable agile engineering action to be an effective lever to improve business processes whilst maintaining ethical standards. The secret is to develop prompts that are geared towards achieving business objectives, do not violate user privacy, and conform to the regulatory standards, setting the tone towards the long-term success of the business.

CHAPTER 9

FUTURE TRENDS IN PROMPT ENGINEERING

Emerging Technologies

In this fast-changing world of modern business technology integration, emerging technologies play a central role in the delivery of a competitive advantage and operational efficiency. With a goal of survival and prosperity, the effort has been geared towards using advances in artificial intelligence, machine learning, and automation, to make processes simpler and decision-making able.

Machine learning has been one of the most relevant technological revolutions that has impacted the global world, especially in artificial intelligence. It provides enterprises with the possibility to process large volumes of information fast and error-free, and derive insights that could not be obtained previously. Companies will be able to predict market trends and consumer behavior more accurately because machine learning algorithms can find patterns and make inferences. This ability is used to support the process of strategic planning and to increase customer engagement through personalizing interactions into predictive analytics.

Automation is another pillar of emerging technologies, and this has changed the manner in which businesses operate since it requires less manual processing of repetitive functions. Automation of routine processes will help companies free human resources to more strategic tasks that cannot be done by computers, and need imagination and analysis. Such a move is not only more productive but also makes errors less likely, hence the output is more harmonious and of high quality.

The introduction of the Internet of Things (IoT) has also increased the scope of opportunities for businesses. IoT also allows real-time data to be collected and analyzed so that the business can drive efficiency and innovation. As an example, in supply chain management, IoT devices may monitor and optimize the supply chain logistics, minimizing the time of a delay and increasing coordination of various supply chain levels.

The second newer tool is Blockchain technology, which is making gains against the prospect of increasing business transactions' security and transparency. Blockchain will allow the maintenance of the integrity of the data, which is essential in sectors that require trust, like finance and healthcare. The technology not only protects sensitive information but also makes transactions more efficient in that there will be less reliance on transactional intermediaries.

In addition, the combination of virtual and augmented reality in operations is creating new opportunities for treating customers and training them. The technologies offer immersive sensations, which can add value to product demonstrations and employee training, and improve product knowledge retention and engagement. In retail, virtual reality has the potential to develop virtual showrooms, which can enable customers to view products in a virtualised scenario prior to a purchase.

Since businesses are still looking to experiment and embrace these new technologies, it is important to discuss the issues that come with their adoption. The concerns of data privacy, cybersecurity, and the ethical application of technology have to be addressed so that the positive change related to technological progress can be achieved without undermining trustworthiness and security.

It can be summarized by saying that the incorporation of emergent technologies into business practices is not only a trend but a must to stay in tune with a fast-paced world. The strength of artificial intelligence, automation, IoT, blockchain, and virtual reality can help businesses harness previously untapped levels of efficiency and innovation, and the result will be not only lasting success but also further expansion in the digital era.

Predicting Industry Shifts

In the fast-moving world of business, anticipating industry changes is not just an added advantage but a must in the long run.

Knowing how to read the micro-movements in an industry environment can give companies a considerable competitive advantage with which they can adjust their strategies, invent new product lines, or reprioritize their operation to reflect new trends. This insight into the dynamics of the industry is being promoted by the developments in the field of artificial intelligence and machine learning that can analyze masses of data and foresee changes with high precision.

The blistering technological and digital landscape has changed the way businesses are carried out, and this means that leaders must keep up with these changes. Predictive analytics, through AI, is an important tool in this context as it enables the organization to filter the old analysis and predict trends. Such an ability is invaluable in such industries as finance, retail, and manufacturing, and may guide strategic planning and investment that nurtures consumer behavior and market demand.

Not only that, but adding AI to business processes can increase the ability to identify early warning signs of change. To take a specific example, retailing: the application of AI can monitor buying trends and customer reviews, with the effect that it can inform changes in consumer needs well before they become reflected in the actual sales data. This allows enterprises to optimize their stock holding and marketing initiatives before it is too late to avoid reasons of dead tonnage and maximize promotions.

Besides consumer trends, there is also a need to predict the changes in the industry by comprehending regulatory shifts and technological innovations. Businesses have to remain updated on possible regulatory effects and innovations that may threaten the current business model. AI can help to scan worldwide regulatory conditions and technology shifts, offering notifications of shifts that may impact operations. Indicatively, changes in regulatory requirements in the automotive sector, such as the need to meet changes in emission levels or the development of electric cars, can be the determining factors for whether a business strategy is going well or failing badly.

Moreover, the ability to have scenario planning and simulation using AI allows businesses to take into consideration multiple futures. Companies can develop simulations of different scenarios with a high level of detail and simulate the effects of the various strategies to develop contingencies for different events. Such a strategy not only makes businesses ready to face any disruptions but also enables them to exploit opportunities where others fail to see any.

The role of a leader in this prophetic exercise is hard to overestimate. Leaders need to instill a culture of agility and lifelong learning at their enterprises and teach their teams to be open to data-backed decisions and innovation. By building up a culture where predictive analytics insights are not only welcome but also incorporated into the strategic plans, the business in question will be able to stay resilient and proactive.

To sum up, anticipation of the changes that impact the industry is one of the crucial elements of the contemporary business strategy. With AI and data analysis, it is possible to predict and be ready to transform and keep the marketplace. The use of predictive tools within the business workflow helps not only predict the trends on the market but also allows aligning the business objectives with the surrounding industry, which guarantees long-term success within the business field.

Preparing for the Future

In a world where the rate of technological change is unrelenting, businesses should develop a flexible strategic approach to immediate engineering to keep in line with the existing and emerging trends. Strategic foresight becomes central and involves the annual strategy meetings, whereby emphasis is placed on horizon scanning and scenario planning with a view to predicting changes in the landscape in a bid to stay within the bigger business objectives. This strategy is not only defensive but actively plans out a strategy to expand on the already promising libraries and combine novel tools, thereby ensuring that the enterprise stays ahead of the curve when it comes to the latest in AI-based innovations.

The key aspect of future-proofing entails the smooth interrelation of timely engineering with the overall concept of digital transformation and the enhancement of talents. It requires the establishment of cross-functional collaborations, especially with IT, Human Resources, and Learning and Development departments, to bake in timely engineering as a pillar in the company's digital skills framework. Such integration makes sure that prompt engineering is not cornered but is built into the organizational operations and strategies.

Frequent technology and process auditing is crucial to this strategic approach towards futureproofing. Scheduled platform reviews, check-ins, and compliance audits are some of the audits that should occur regularly to ensure that they remain relevant and effective. They also give the outline to consider the feedback and the creation of continuous improvement in the prompt engineering processes.

It is important to take an open-minded and fast approach as new use cases of AI present themselves. The trial of new models, tools, or timely methodology has to be endorsed by leadership, but it should encourage a culture of change and innovation tolerance. Regular executive briefings on AI can become very helpful in terms of knowledge updates on current market trends and the occurrence of technological advances, thus offering leaders the information they need to make quality decisions.

Several examples explain how to develop resilience and adaptability, where an organization needs to foster a culture of experimentation and safe failure. That includes the construction of environments in which iterative testing is promoted, and innovation can be achieved by learning through errors. This kind of culture is buttressed by a message from the leaders who esteem experimenting, setting examples, and being rewarded for thoughtful innovativeness.

Besides internal strategies, it is also important to remain updated with external resources. Businesses must also be proactive in connecting with credible online prompt libraries and the AI community, so they stay current on the latest trends and best practices. This involvement not only increases its capabilities internally but also helps improve its position in the field of prompt engineering.

The real issue of preparing for the future in prompt engineering is to create a strong, versatile framework adapted to the changes in the technological environment. It implies long-term thinking, inter-establishment cooperation, continuous auditing, and an environment of learning and innovation. The integration of these principles into their core business processes enables organizations not only to future-proof their business strategies but also to enable environmentally-friendly long-term growth and ensure that they have a competitive edge in the fast-growing realm of AI.

Long-term Strategic Planning

Strategic planning in the business world is one of the most important tools that leads organizations to success in the long run. The chapter examines the complexity of the long-term strategic planning process, which is crucial in planning business goals in line with the dynamic market environment.

The key feature of a successful strategic planning is the intersection of anticipating and adjusting to the future. This requires a thorough knowledge of internal capacities and external market conditions. By doing a robust market analysis and a competitor analysis, businesses can find the opportunities and threats. Such planning enables organizations to place themselves in a favorable position by capitalizing on their advantages and reducing the risks that may be involved.

A strategic planning element is goal setting, which should be specific and measurable. The goals have worked as a guide, which can direct the effort of the organization; they are a form of roadmap that the organization uses to determine where to channel its resources. Such goals should be ambitious and realistic to enable the organization to stretch its capacity without being out of reach in the specified period of time.

Part of drafting a strategic plan is coordination with different departments. Departments have diverse knowledge and skill sets that contribute to the overall picture of how the organization stands and what it can accomplish. The potential of this joint effort is that the plan will be holistic and will take into consideration every aspect of the business, including operations and finance, marketing, and human resources functions, among others.

Monitoring and evaluation are required in the implementation of a strategic plan. Frequent assessment enables the organization to monitor progress, and where there are changes to the plan, appropriate changes can be made. Such a repetitive exercise is essential in ensuring the response to the set objectives as well as adjusting to any unpredictable alterations in the marketing environment.

In addition, strategic planning is a dynamic activity and not a one-off event. The business environment is dynamic, and the organization must be able to change its strategy to keep up with the dynamism. This flexibility makes the organization relevant and competitive, thus able to tap new opportunities and evade challenges as they appear.

The human component of long-term strategic planning is an all too often-neglected factor. Employees must be engaged and inspired to pursue the strategic vision. It can be done via clear communication, compatibility between the individual roles and organizational objectives, and a culture of innovation and continuous improvement.

In the highly dynamic world that we live in today, technology has a very crucial role to play in strategic planning. Combining advanced analytics and artificial intelligence into the mix can present even more valuable insights since it can supplement decision-making processes, helping organizations make more accurate predictions. Such a technological power will boost the competition, enabling business firms to remain at the edge.

As a practical matter, long-term strategic planning involves the establishment of a long-term sustainable future for the organization. It is about making the right decisions today that will lead to success tomorrow. By showing a clear vision, collaborative effort, and adaptability, organizations will be able to navigate the complicated structure of the business world and reach a period of success.

CHAPTER 10

TROUBLESHOOTING AND OPTIMIZATION

Common Issues and Solutions

In the arena of prompt engineering, which is fast changing, the companies involved frequently face a sequence of general issues that may seriously influence the effectiveness of the AI-powered products. Its insignificance or lack of consistency is another common complication because conversational AI may offer choppy tones, random subjects, missing information, or variation in response lengths. Such discrepancies are frequently the result of inappropriate design of prompts, poor quality of inputs, or model flaws.

In order to diagnose and correct these dilemmas, it is important to gather and study a variety of outputs obtained for the same prompt. This is achieved by collecting a minimum of five different responses in order to define trends and anomalies. This can be aided by creating a "prompt output log" of repetitive tasks that may assist in diagnosing patterns that can be adjusted in prompt design or data input.

Environmental and contextual factors are also very crucial in terms of output reliability. AI performance can be impacted by changes in model versions, platform updates, data source inconsistencies, and so on. The speed of prompt delivery, word counts, and tokens, and session history can also have a big impact on the ways in which outputs may be affected. It will require a formalized method of root cause analysis where one variable at a time is isolated and assessed prior to any change being implemented.

When prompts do not produce the desired outcomes, a logical method of troubleshooting may be worthwhile. The first is to reconsider the prompt and make it clear and concrete, and free of ambiguity or lack of adequate context. With minimum input and subsequent addition of greater complexity, it becomes possible to assess which 3DK prompts the issue. Some of the common prompt problems, like unclear instructions, unstructured responses, and poor business context, can be addressed by making instructions clear, describing the required response, and providing the business context.

It is advisable to develop an all-encompassing checklist that would contain strategies to deal with these problems. The questions that may be put in this checklist are: "Is the action verb clear?", "Have you set boundaries for the AI?" and "Is the prompt too long?" Further, escalation considerations and points should be laid down to channel escalations to technical or compliance units. Some examples include IT penetration, which may be required in case of bugs in the platform, and legal consultation on sensitive outputs.

Another important step in keeping the AI-generated content accurate, relevant, and compliant is output validation. Some quality control through human review, such as compliance checks, before use in the business, may assure that an AI output meets business-specific standards. These can be factual correctness, alignment with business, legal, and brand requirements. High risks are associated with cross-functional review loops with legal or compliance checks or those involving subject-matter experts.

Lastly, through safe experimentation, it is possible to achieve large gains in AI performance by iteratively refining the prompts. This includes working with a sandbox environment to test new prompts and to perform structured A/B testing to compare prompt variants. Instead, iterations during development are documented and tracked, there is a changelog, and the culture is instilled to learn through errors. By focusing on such frequently occurring challenges and introducing systematic solutions to them, organizations can unlock all the benefits of AI in pursuit of improved productivity and overall success.

Optimizing for Performance

In the business world, where speed and accuracy are everything, performance optimization in prompt engineering is a craft that combines innovation with strategic planning. The underlying advantage of such optimization is that it makes it possible to refine the prompts to maximum effectiveness and relevance in a business network. This elaborate process should commence with a proper understanding of the business goal and the particular tasks that will be automated or improved by AI-based prompts.

The way to optimization begins by dividing a single, compound business task into smaller and more manageable segments that can be solved separately with the help of carefully designed prompts. That means tediously dissecting activities, with the goal of determining the most material factors that can then be converted into things that can be prompted. An example of this is that the task of streamlining customer service can be broken down into promptable elements that include writing personalized customer responses, summarizing customer communication, and developing follow-up actions.

To formulate specific prompts, one has to pay close attention to detail and be sensitive to the words being written. The instructions that follow the prompts have to be clear, as they should be written in action words with a description of the preferred format and length of the expected paper. By establishing such parameters, businesses can make sure that AI produces outputs that are not just right but also embedded within the needs specific to the particular task.

In addition, it is important to provide relevant background information to ensure high-quality results through contextualization of prompts. This would involve giving the AI the needed constraints and exclusions to help the AI produce relevant and useful outputs. As an example, when ordering a sales report, the specification not to include a weekend would instruct the AI to eliminate all the weekend activities and present a report that only reflects weekday activities, which makes the information presented highly pertinent.

The importance of example-based prompts, or few-shot learning, can hardly be overestimated in tuning performance. The possibility of doing this is by feeding the AI with examples of inputs and outputs expected, and hence, the quality of the responses generated would be significantly enhanced. The approach will enable the AI to learn based on particular examples and evolve its actions to suit the unique demands of various business situations.

Avoiding AI hallucinations, when the model gives inaccurate or wrong information, is another significant factor related to performance optimization. These risks can be mitigated by using such techniques as asking the AI to use only the data presented and establishing rather stringent boundaries. Also, to approve the final outputs, a human-in-the-loop process for validation will be applied to certify that the results are within the defined standards of accuracy and compliance.

Optimization can also include significant improvement by means of repeated testing and feedback loops. By keeping a record of timely output and examining patterns, businesses will be able to identify places for improvement and implement them. It is this iterative process that is critical towards evolving to changing business needs and technology developments, to maintain that prompt engineering is an ever-evolving process.

The key takeaway in performance optimization in terms of prompt engineering is that the most demanded is not only increased efficiency but also business empowerment with AI potential. By optimizing prompts around business objectives, organizations can access previously inaccessible levels of productivity and creativity and remain at the cutting-edge of AI-enabled business.

Continuous Improvement

Under continuous improvement, an organization has no choice but to maintain continuous improvement in the field of prompt engineering to experience sustained results in business applications. It is in this continuous process that the relevance and thus the effective performance of the prompt-driven strategies remain relevant, as organizations today are able to adapt to the changing nature of artificial intelligence and its implementation.

The basis of continuous improvement in prompt engineering is the systematic performance analysis and optimization of available prompts. This includes a process of regular review whereby prompts are measured by looking at their effectiveness in bringing out desired results. Along with the accuracy of the outputs, such an assessment should also take into consideration their correlation with the areas of business, policies of compliance, and the changing needs of the organization. In that way, companies can determine where prompts are lacking and where they need improvement.

Another major element of this iterative process is the gathering and assessment of feedback from several stakeholders, such as business leaders and end-users. Such a feedback loop is critical in gaining an insight into how prompts work in practical contexts and in areas that need improvement. By creating an organizational culture that values open communication and critical feedback, one can be sure that his or her prompt engineering practices will be adaptable to and embarking on change.

In addition, the constant increase in the speed of work on engineering requirements requires an active approach to learning and growth. This includes keeping up with the most current improvements in artificial intelligence and machine learning technology and comprehending how these changes can be used to increase quick performance. Businesses ought to invest in education so that their employees have the capabilities to accommodate new tools and techniques. This vow to post-graduate learning can help not only in increasing the competence of each member of the team but also in the organizational capacity to manage complex AI-based responsibilities.

Other than internal transformation initiatives, organizations must also look down the ecosystem, seeking ways through which they can collaborate and share knowledge with industry peers. Getting involved in AI communities, attending conferences, and connecting with thought leaders can offer some great ideas on best practices and new trends. Combining these outside insights and views with internal strategies will enable the companies to develop a more balanced view of prompt engineering that is both creative and based on industry standards.

The incorporation of effective assessment metrics and KPIs to gauge the achievement of timely applications also comes in as another important factor in continuous improvement. One should design these metrics in a manner that captures not only quantitative performance but also qualitative performance of such metrics, e.g., user satisfaction and alignment with strategic objectives. Due to metrics evaluation on a regular basis, the organizations will be able to picture the efficiency of their timely engineering and decide on future deliberations.

Lastly, constant improvement needs to be viewed as a repetitive process where evaluation and refinement are newer cycles that add to the previous cycles. Such an iterative quality helps promote experimentation and readiness to accept change, which is crucial to innovation. Incorporating continuous improvement within the inner processes of their business, the organizations can make sure that their immediate engineering plans will be efficient, up-to-date, and able to provide their companies with visible business returns in the long run.

Feedback Loops

Feedback loops can be defined as an important part of the dynamic world of the business, where they can be improved and innovated continuously. It is one of the building blocks in the formulation of a prompt engineering strategy since organizations are able to polish and be grounded in the actual outcomes and experiences. The immediate feedback loops are central to a culture of irritation and adaptation, a learning process that has to be performed in a fast-changing world of AI and immediate engineering.

The merging and interpretation of data created as a result of AI contact lies at the centre of the feedback loops. This data will offer invaluable insights into the performance and effectiveness of prompts. They will show which prompts can lead to the desired outcomes and which prompts need to be modified to achieve the corrections. Through a systematic collection of feedback from different sources, such as end-users and stakeholders, and even internal teams, business participants can develop trends and tendencies, helping them to make corrections and consolidations promptly.

Among the main advantages of feedback loops, one should mention the possibility of increasing the accuracy and reasonableness of artificial intelligence products. By repeatedly testing and reworking prompts, organizations can refine the prompts to be effective and targeted towards business objectives and user expectations. Such a process entails not only reviewing the accuracy and clarity of prompts but also reflecting upon some other elements like tone, context, and being compliant with brand guidelines. Feedback loops will enable the constant reorientation of AI outputs to the business-level strategic objectives to maximize their usefulness and effectiveness.

Structured feedback mechanisms play an important role in the process of sustaining effective feedback. This includes the establishment of feedback-gathering channels, including surveys, user reviews, and performance analytics. These channels must be set up to capture an extended amount of insight, including things like technical performance data and qualitative user responses. With the use of powerful analytics tools, companies can turn the raw feedback into insights, thus leading to timely changes and improvements in response.

Furthermore, the feedback loops can create a collaborative environment whereby cross-functional teams can add value to the timely engineering process. Engaging a wider range of minds means that organizations can utilize a great depth of knowledge and experience, thus encouraging innovativeness and creation. Feedback done collectively (through workshops and hackathons, for example) fosters the sharing of ideas and suggestions, which results in stronger and more versatile prompt solutions.

Besides improving existing prompts, feedback loops are also pretty important in the creation of novel prompts. By reviewing the reception of their past iterations, organizations can see what needs to be answered and what trends tend to emerge, and in turn use this information to draft new prompts that will answer those needs. This is a proactive strategy that leads to businesses being nimble and adaptive to changing walkways and consumer desires.

In a bid to maximize the effectiveness of feedback loops, openness and transparency should be created. Inviting feedback and sharing the experiences among the team members by showing them that mistakes are welcome to be seen as the sources of improvement, encourages the team to promote a learning-oriented environment. Celebrating successful prompt improvements and having this as a part of recognition can also encourage teams to be engaged in the feedback process.

In short, feedback loops can be an extremely useful methodology to increase the level of efficiency and flexibility of timely engineering solutions. By inculcating these loops within the fabric of their operations, businesses will be in a position to make sure that their AI-related activities are continuously primed and aligned with their strategic priorities. Such a feedback and iteration cycle not only leads to innovation but also enables companies to get the full value out of AI as a business asset.

CHAPTER 11

PROMPT ENGINEERING IN MARKETING

Crafting Persuasive Campaigns

In the fast-moving business environment, campaign writing is a very important skill. The core of every great campaign is the ability to comprehend and to manipulate human behavior with properly used messaging. An effective campaign cannot be based solely on what you say because it has to do with how you say it, when you say it, and to whom it is said. The nature of a persuasive campaign lies in its capability to hit a chord with the audience on both emotional and intellectual levels, thus driving them to choose the required action.

The crucial move toward the creation of a persuasive campaign is to have a good understanding of the target audience. This means investigating their needs, wants, and pain points. Building an audience profile will enable businesses to focus their messaging on the issues and needs of their customers. Such a high degree of personalization not only maximizes engagement but also leads to the feeling of being more connected to the brand as well as trust.

After comprehending, the next step is to clarify the relaying of a clear and persuasive message. This will summarize the value proposition of the product or service, and point out what is different and special about it. The message must be conveyed in a manner that is understandable and easy to remember, with terms that are both reachable and understood by the target market. The power of storytelling may come in useful in this case, as the stories can connect and convince, allowing the brand to make its message more personified and moving.

The time and context are also important ingredients in an argument. A message, which lands at the right time and in the right context, will increase its effectiveness significantly. Having a clear picture of the customer journey and strategically inserting messages at the right points can encourage customers to take the required action. This may include the deployment of data analytics to understand the best times and platforms on which the message will reach the audience in the most likely circumstances to listen to the message.

Moreover, the selection of channels is key to ensuring that the campaign has the utmost reach and effect. Using the wide range of digital channels available today, it is necessary to choose the correct combination of channels. Be it social media, email marketing, or content marketing, each channel possesses different strengths and has the potential to be used to attract different value segments of the audience. A multi-channel strategy can be used to remind the message on touchpoints and heighten the chances of conversion.

The last element in creating a convincing campaign is ongoing testing and tuning. By monitoring the performance of the campaign in terms of engagement rates, conversion rates, and customer feedback, businesses will be able to determine what works and what needs to be improved. This is a data-driven strategy where any necessary adjustments can be made in real-time, making the given campaign relevant throughout its lifespan.

To sum it up, persuasive campaign creation is a complex process that demands a thorough study of the target audience, a unique and eloquent message, proper timing and habitat, selection of the channels, and constant and continuous enhancement. When businesses learn to master these factors, they will be in a position to develop campaigns that will not only capture attention but will also elicit specific action needed to help reach business success.

Using AI for Market Analysis

Market analysis is a key competitive advantage strategy in the fast-changing business environment that uses AI to gain a competitive edge. With artificial intelligence and analytics embedded in the market analysis systems, companies can analyze large amounts of data in record time and in an accurate manner. Such ability not only increases the correctness of estimating conditions on the market but also provides opportunities to realize real-time insights, which may be important in making strategic decisions.

The role started by IA in market analysis is its capabilities in processing and analyzing humongous amounts of data that are put to diverse uses. More conventional market analysis techniques tend to use fixed reports and past data that may soon become obsolete in the modern world of high-speed market conditions. Unlike people, AI systems can digest and analyse new data in real time, giving businesses real-time insight. With this dynamic analysis, companies can recognize the arising trends and changes in consumer behavior much quickly than ever before.

Besides, AI has strong powers in pattern recognition, which is fundamental in market analysis. Such systems have the capacity to detect weak trends and correlations in the data that human analysts can miss. As an example, AI can identify shifts in consumer sentiment, looking at posts on social media and online reviews, and provide companies with a more detailed picture of how consumers feel about their products or services. This will come in quite handy as far as predicting market changes and acting on them.

The second key benefit of the market analysis using AI is that it also predicts. AI can predict market trends in the future through machine learning algorithms and historical data being fed into an AI. This predictive power is such an invaluable asset to businesses in terms of making strategies, be it on the introduction of a new product, a new market, or a price strategy. AI-infused predictive analytics can guide a business not only to react to the shifts in the market but also to anticipate them, which creates a competitive edge.

Additionally, greater marketing personalization is possible with the help of AI. Artificial intelligence can be used to analyze customer data and segment customer bases more finely, creating customer-based marketing campaigns within specific audiences based on consumer behavior and preference. This personalisation adds value to the marketing process and customer interaction, thus leading to a sale and customer loyalty.

Nonetheless, there are many challenges associated with the incorporation of AI in market analysis. Companies have to be sure that high-quality and relevant data is supplied to their AI systems to present proper insights. There is also a demand for human expertise, i.e., one that is capable of addressing the processed data that is generated by the AI and incorporating the inferences in the strategic decision-making procedures. Nevertheless, Artificial Intelligence in market Analysis presents helpful reimbursement, and we should not ignore its assistance in conducting market analysis.

Finally, AI usage in market analysis offers a paradigm shift in how businesses comprehend and react to the movements in the marketplace. With the use of AI, organizations can gain a better, more vivid insight into the market trends, thus making rational business decisions that will lead to increased profitability. With the further development of AI technology, its mechanism is likely to become even more significant in market analysis. It will potentially provide more advanced tools for companies to utilize on their way to success.

Personalization at Scale

In the contemporary business world, the ability to personalize encounters and experiences is critical. Personalization at scale can be viewed as one of the most transformational strategies, as it helps to serve an enormous number of people and make their experience personalized. This strategy will utilize the power of very new technologies, especially AI/ data analytics, that will help to provide the most unique experiences without the restriction of traditional practices.

Behind all of personalization at scale is a capacity to collect and process huge quantities of data. These types of data, which may range from client interactions, their purchase histories, and their behavioral trends, are extremely vital in gaining insight into the personal preferences and forecasting future actions. AI tools are particularly important in the efficient processing of such data, pattern identification, and the drawing of insights in an actionable way. The insights allow companies to produce very individual marketing campaigns, product recommendations, and customer service that will appeal to the individual consumer.

Engagement and retention of customers are two of the main strengths of personalization at scale. By giving people experiences that resonate as meaningful, businesses will create deeper emotional ties with the customer, resulting in greater customer loyalty and satisfaction. This customer-centered interaction is not confined to marketing, but also all aspects of the customers, such as support, sales, and after-sales matters. For example, emails sent out in customers' names and possibly containing product suggestions based on previously made purchases have a better open rate and conversion rate than general emails.

In addition to this, personalization as a mass practice allows enterprises to maximize their operations and resource deployment. Through the knowledge of the preferences and behaviours of the customers, companies have a better ability to predict demand, and that reduces the wastage in the management of inventory. This speed also increases the satisfaction of the customer, but it also adds to the viability of the whole business activity.

Nonetheless, executing personalization on a large scale is not an easy task. The major obstacle is the preservation of data privacy and security. Businesses are required to ensure they abide by strict regulations and ethics when handling and analyzing consumers' personal information. Transparency in the use of data and seeking consent from the user is a requisite practice to create trust and meet and maintain the requirements of the law, like GDPR and CCPA.

The next difficulty is the aggregation of the personalization tactics in various platforms and touchpoints. Organizations need to make sure that their personalization initiatives are harmonious and integrated to give a unified experience to the customer, no matter the channel being used to access it. This entails the strong interconnection of data systems and the harmonization of the efforts of various sections of an organization.

Finally, personalization at scale is a tremendous business opportunity to gain a more competitive advantage in a busy market. With data-driven insights and access to superior AI technologies, businesses can provide each customer with an experience that will not only exceed but also satisfy their needs. Technology is portrayed to keep evolving, and along with these shifts, a greater reach of personalization will be possible, providing new opportunities to innovate and even expand. The benefits to companies that are ready to adopt such a strategy are enormous. They can mean higher customer satisfaction, better operational performance, and therefore higher profits.

Tracking Marketing ROI

In the world of contemporary commerce, the capacity to follow up and determine marketing ROI with precision is the clue. This is initiated by the formulation of clear, quantifiable objectives in line with business objectives. With such benchmarks, organizations will be in a position to determine the effectiveness of their marketing plans towards generating quantifiable outcomes. Marketing ROI is not just a success indicator, but a diagnostic tool that leads to adaptation of the campaigns in order to maximize the impact.

The initial phase in marketing ROI tracking is to set the key performance indicators (KPIs) that will signify the desired results. Such KPIs have to be both specific and measurable, and they are to include lead generation, conversion rates, customer acquisition costs, and retention rates. Clarification of such indicators will help organize the business strategy to be more in line with market objectives.

The next important stage is data collection, and it requires powerful systems that would grasp the important information across all marketing channels. These involve the digital touch points, which include social media interactions, digital emails, and digital analytics on websites, and the traditional media engagements. The combination of these data sets will give them a holistic picture of the customer journey and help them determine which touchpoints play the most powerful roles in conversion.

After the data collection process is over, comes the analysis part, whereby companies will have to sift through the massive information to be able to identify patterns and insights. Advanced analytical tools can help a great deal in this process since they can allow marketers to detect trends, correlate activities with outcomes, and even see the reasoning behind consumer behaviors. The analysis can assist not only in current performance evaluation quantity but also in predicting future patterns and prospects.

One of the most important factors when monitoring marketing ROI is the attribution model, which is used to allocate value to given marketing activities. Multi-touch attribution models are gaining popularity because they consider multiple interactions that the consumer goes through prior to making a purchase. The models serve as a more differentiated view of the role played by various marketing channels leading to the final sale, and this enables a business to deploy resources more productively.

At the same time, lifetime value (LTV), as a term, has a considerable influence on the measurement of marketing ROI. LTV is the total revenue that a company could receive throughout the period of the customer relationship. When calculated, LTV can help the business become more aware of the potential long-term effects that any form of marketing will have. Therefore, the customer acquisition strategies applied should be sustainable and profitable.

The last element of tracking marketing ROI is constant development of strategies on the basis of knowledge obtained from consumer analysis. This is an iterative process of experimenting and improving many aspects of marketing campaigns, including but not limited to messaging and targeting, ultimately channel selection, and budget allocation. This employs a spirit of experimentation and adjustment to make businesses adaptable and quick to the changes in the market, as the customers want.

Ultimately, ROI marketing tracking is an evolvable exercise that draws a combination of strategy, analytical, and creative skills. It is all about leveraging data to make informed decisions so that marketing efforts are not only geared to deliver short-term goals but also lead to the long-term flourishing and prosperity of the organization. In the current marketing environment, where businesses have to deal with numerous marketing variations and changes, the capacity to monitor and optimize ROI is essential to compete favorably.

CHAPTER 12

PROMPT ENGINEERING FOR CUSTOMER SUPPORT

Automating Responses

In the context of contemporary business, the capability to automate an answer effectively is revolutionizing the way companies operate with their clients and organize their in-house procedures. Response automation raw means running responses based on artificial intelligence (AI) that automates repetitive tasks to free human resources to concentrate on more strategic activities. This is not simply a replacement of the role of human interaction but a betterment of the same because responses in this case will be timely, relevant, and consistent.

Automating responses begins with realizing which tasks are repetitive, but imperative to the business activity. These activities usually comprise customer inquiries, normal requests, and internal messages. Automation can help ensure clients and employees are provided with timely and correct information, which will promote customer and employee satisfaction and productivity.

In order to execute automation successfully, companies have to establish clear and consistent prompts to AI systems. These triggers help the AI formulate suitable answers. Writing these prompts includes defining the intended output and the scenario that the response shall serve. For example, an auto-response message sent by customer care may require certain products and service protocols to ensure the response is within company policies and customers' expectations.

The other major consideration is how to integrate the AI tools into the established business systems. Integrating AI with customer relationship management (CRM) systems or help desk systems will allow the business to automate the process of reacting to the information based on live data, which makes the information given on time and relevant. Such an integration, besides enhancing the accuracy of response, also aids in tracking and analysis of the customer interaction that, in turn, leads to helpful information to be used to enhance further.

In addition, the automation of responses necessitates installing feedback mechanisms so that the AI's performance can be constantly tuned and improved. This means reviewing how successful automated responses are and taking corrective action on the prompts or training data. Companies also need to design the procedures for managing exceptions when human input has to be made, and computerization must not overshadow or substitute human decision-making.

The merits of automating responses are numerous. It makes businesses work more effectively as there is less time and energy wasted on routine jobs. It also increases or improves customer satisfaction as it offers fast and even responses that are important in this fast-paced market competition. Moreover, it allows employees to concentrate on more challenging and imaginative tasks, leading to the creation and strain development.

In brief, automation of responses is a business tactic that can bring serious improvements to the operations. By strategically choosing what to automate, creating accurate prompts, ensuring that AI systems work together with their existing systems, and establishing feedback patterns, businesses are able to make sure that automation initiatives deliver better efficiency and customer satisfaction. This not only streamlines the workflow but also puts the business in a place where they are quick to respond to the changing market demands, thus ensuring the future success of the business.

Improving Customer Satisfaction

In business, customer satisfaction is one of the most important pillars that can determine the success of the company. Customer service is one of the areas where the integration of the AI-driven prompt engineering has proven to be a revolutionary means of achieving improved customer satisfaction. With the use of advanced algorithms, companies can optimize customer interactions to suit the individual needs and preferences of each customer and help create a more tailored experience.

AI implementation on prompts offers the possibility to automate and improve customer interactions, making them not only faster but also relevant contextually. This ability helps provide a high level of accuracy in addressing frequent customer concerns and questions that otherwise could be a challenge to respond to accurately with manual operations. As an example, customer data can be analyzed by AI to make predictions about any possible problems and ways of addressing them, leading to a drastic decrease in frustration and an improvement in satisfaction.

Furthermore, AI-based prompts can help customer support teams immensely when it comes to efficiency. The automation of the routine queries, as well as the provision of support agents with real-time suggestions, relieves the strain on the human operators, leaving more complicated cases to be handled by humans. This would not only promote the morale and productivity levels of their supporting employees but also improve the level of customer service in general.

The flexibility of AI prompts is also vital to enhancing customer satisfaction. By relying on AI software, the level of customer experience can be amended and polished as it adapts and changes. This is to make sure that customer service is relevant and effective so that they maintain a high level of customer satisfaction.

Moreover, the application of AI to customer related conversations assists in collecting informative data, which may be utilized in the further enhancement of customer-service policies. Understanding trends and customer feedback in light of the customer interactions, companies can quickly recognize improvement points and institute specific interventions to improve the customer experience.

Another aspect that should be reviewed is the role of AI in offering a fluctuating brand voice during customer interactions. Integrating brand instructions into AI prompts helps companies to guarantee that any interaction a customer can have with them is maintained, adhering to their brand positioning. This uniformity is critical in the development of trust and loyalty in customers.

Although the benefits of AI are massive, businesses need to keep the balance between automation and human interaction. Although AI can cover a vast scope of work, there are situations where empathy and judgment given by a human can be really needed. Therefore, a hybrid model that takes into account the advantages of AI and presents them with human supervision can become an optimal customer service plan.

Finally, with AI-driven prompt engineering, customer satisfaction can potentially be greatly increased through a thoughtful application of this approach to customer service. By improving the speed, accuracy, and personalization of customer interactions, the businesses can not only actually meet but also exceed. Still, they will even exceed the expectations of the customers, thus creating long-term success and loyalty to the business. The companies that understand the potential of AI in customer service and successfully apply it in their processes are bound to obtain a competitive advantage in the market.

Reducing Response Times

In this high-stress and fast-moving world of business, the capacity to act quickly on the requests and solicitations of the customer, as well as other operational issues, may make the difference between a successful and a failing company. With regard to this, one of the priorities that companies must observe in order to become highly efficient and satisfy customers involves the minimization of response times. And the golden nugget of this initiative is the strategic application of AI-guided prompt engineering that promises an evolutionary solution to streamlining response workflows.

Companies are now awash with a plethora of requests and assignments that should be addressed immediately. Whether it is responding to customer support requests or internal decision-making mechanisms, the rate at which they are handled can be a critical determinant of performance as well as the view of the clients towards the business. Using the power of AI, organizations are able to automate these processes and speed them up, creating a situation where the time lag commonly associated with human input can be minimized.

Prompt engineering plays a significant role in this transformation. It entails the development of fine-grained and contextually sensitive prompts that will lead AI systems to produce the correct and pertinent responses within a small amount of time. The bottom line of effective prompt engineering is to be able to reduce intricate questions or tasks into simple instructions that an AI can react to effectively. This not only accelerates the response time but also improves the accuracy and relevance of the outputs.

The first such benefit is that when response time is shorter due to AI, it can manage higher numbers of inquiries without compromising quality. As another example, AI-powered applications in the context of customer support can sort through requests and prioritize accordingly, so that critical ones get the immediate attention they deserve. This not only increases customer satisfaction but also helps to relieve the human agent of the burden of working on straightforward queries, with them focusing more on the complex queries that require the human touch.

Furthermore, deployment of AI in the response cycles helps businesses to run 24/7 to support and make decisions continuously. This is very helpful to international firms with clients in other parts of the world. By guaranteeing an immediate reply and delivery of these replies, business establishments are able to provide a standard level of service regardless of space and time factors.

The incorporation of prompt engineering enables more building of knowledge bases and systems that are capable of learning and adapting in the long-term process. The responses obtained and the results received can be analyzed in order to improve the ways AI systems do their work; they will be more efficient and effective in processing queries. This iteration of improvement is critical to being able to manage the speed of change in the business.

Nevertheless, there are some obstacles to the shift to AI-driven prompt engineering. It is necessary to ensure that AI systems learn using correct and extensive data to eliminate inaccuracies and bias in the answers. Also, having a balance between automation and human control is vital in ensuring that the AI systems adopt the company values and expectations of the customers.

In short, minimising response time courtesy of prompt engineering is not simply about speeding up processes but reinventing methods of how business organizations must speak to their customers and mould internal workflow. It is one of the signs of the transition to a more proactive, efficient, and customer-centric business model, and it relies on the strengths of AI to address the needs of the contemporary market. The faster businesses are able to react and act, the better they will fare within this digital age of businesses because speed is one of the most defining attributes of a successful business.

Measuring Support Success

Measurement of support mechanism efficiency is paramount in the context of prompt engineering, where AI-based solutions are supposed to bring concrete gains to corporations. This is not the ordinary understanding of success because the main emphasis is not on how the customer service complaints are attended to promptly; this has been analyzed in a wider view to look at how an entire mechanism can utilize the customer service concept to reflect aspects of the whole business strategy, at the same time, not compromising on customer satisfaction.

First is the definition of key performance indicators (KPIs), which means the definition of success. Such metrics must be tied to the overall business goals, including enhancing customer satisfaction, lowering response times, and first-contact resolution rates. Clear and measurable goals allow businesses to monitor progress and see the spots that need to be improved.

This is one of the ways of evaluating support success by surveying the opinions and satisfaction of customers. This kind of tool gives direct information on the perceptions and experiences of the customer, and thus, a business can know its strong and weak areas in support operations. Tracing a trend in customer responses over a time period can identify trends that can be used to identify underlying system problems, or to show practices that are working that can be replicated throughout the organization.

The issue of measuring the success of support is to evaluate the efficiency of operations. This involves measuring the performance indicators like the average handling time, ticket resolution rates, and the number of support requests that were completed per duration. Above par performance in these regions tends to be interconnected with thoroughly optimized support activities and reflects a sound active strategy.

Besides, the success of support can be evaluated by reviewing the proficiency of escalation processes. Efficient escalation procedures make sure that a complicated matter is resolved in time by the relevant groups of people, keeping customer angst to a minimum and avoiding the possibility of bottlenecks. The next step would be quantifying the regularity and the treatment outcomes of the escalations, and this would give an idea of the effectiveness of the prevailing support framework and how process improvements can be introduced.

Alongside quantitative indicators, it is important to mention such an aspect as qualitative support measurement. This will be done by looking at the content and tone of the exchange of information between customers and support staff. Businesses can increase customer loyalty and trust by making sure that it is in the brand voice and values and ensuring that communications made are consistent. Such interactions can be developed further through regular training and feedback to support teams in order to result in better customer experiences.

Technology is also the key to measuring the success of the support. Smart analytics can also automate support collection and analysis to deliver real-time insights and make advanced adjustments to support plans. These tools may also be useful in identifying any tendencies and possible problems that may arise before they develop, and they enable businesses to offer a high level of support.

Lastly, improvement should be regularly experienced in a bid to maintain support success. This means continually updating and redefining supporting processes, using new technologies, and responding to the new demands of customers. Continuous learning and innovation will allow businesses to have effective support operations in line with their strategic objectives.

To conclude, a combination approach should measure success in support of prompt engineering; quantitative and qualitative measures should be combined. ABC businesses aimed at high customer satisfaction, efficiency, and continuous improvement can develop support structures that would not only resolve issues but would also bring long-term success and customer loyalty.

CHAPTER 13

PROMPT ENGINEERING FOR HR AND RECRUITMENT

Streamlining Hiring Processes

In the ever-changing environment of human resources, efficiency and accuracy in the hiring process are now at a premium. Organizations are going to innovations to cope with the huge number of applications and resumes they get. The application of AI-powered prompt engineering in the hiring process is revolutionizing how companies conduct their hiring processes, which presents a much more streamlined, scalable, and objective approach to candidate screening.

In the past, the process of sorting through thousands of resumes to find appropriate people to hire has been a labor-intensive, consuming process. In recruiting, the challenge of speed versus the emphasis of thoroughness is even more overwhelming, especially in recruiting that involves a high percentage of individuals, where the greatest danger is to lose the potential talents, considering the pressure of speed involved in massive recruitment. Such antique methodology not only dissipates resources but also puts recruiters at risk of getting burned out and the possibility of losing a quality candidate due to snap decisions because of human error or prejudice.

The massive wave of applications received by the traditional recruitment systems is a major problem with these systems. As a solution to such problems, prompt engineering carries out a very efficient step in automating the process of screening the resumes most effectively and efficiently. By using AI, organizations can adopt timely templates that are specifically created to scavenge critical qualifications in the resumes paired with red flags. All these templates are designed to identify those skills, experiences, and credentials that will facilitate a more precise ranking of the candidates based on previously determined criteria. Not only does this speed up the preliminary screening process, but it also increases the quality of the short list that is submitted to human talent.

It works by incorporating AI outputs into the current HR workflow. Resumes can be submitted, and after that, the AI system will process them, extracting relevant details and comparing the qualifications of the candidates to the job opening. The speed and accuracy with which the AI can handle large amounts of data ensure that recruiters will have more time to spend on contacts with the potential candidates that deserve their attention, instead of investigating the details of preselecting. This is visually portrayed as a continuous process of AI screening to validation by a recruiter and lastly, to the interview shortlist.

The advantages of such a transformation are high. Organizations are seeing significant improvement in time-to-hire. Not only will this reduce costs, but it will also improve the experience of those applicants, who will receive timelier responses and updates. The advantage of AI in the candidate assessment also ensures less bias in the process of hiring, which encourages a fairer process where non-traditional candidates can be discovered.

The positive impact of AI-driven prompt engineering is highlighted in the feedback received by recruiters who have adopted it. They are more focused and happier at work since their tasks are no longer limited to administrative assignments but rather have become more strategic. Moreover, through data-driven knowledge delivered by AI, the hiring process can be continuously improved so that prompt templates can always keep up with shifting business requirements and market transformations.

In summary, expedited engineering in recruiting is not simply an operational improvement, but it is a business strategy. Automating resume screening and incorporating AI into the recruitment workflow enables organizations to do the same, resulting in an improved, fair, and effective hire. This is one of the technological innovations that are indicative of another stage of adopting HR procedures that are aligned with the overall goals of business prosperity, which enables companies to have the ability to attract and retain the most talented people in an environment that is becoming highly competitive.

Enhancing Employee Engagement

In the busy world of business, employee engagement has turned out to be the key to organizational success. Employee engagement is more than the glitzy bells and whistles of a workplace environment; it is about fostering a long-term sense of belonging and purpose among workers. When the employees are able to feel important and connected to the work that they do, they are likely to put forth their best efforts, which results in increased productivity and innovation.

The best way to cultivate employee engagement is, therefore, first identifying what motivates employees. This starts with creating an open cultural communication and trust. The workers are expected to share their ideas and concerns without any undue feelings that they might be victimized. This transparent communication not only empowers a person but also creates an atmosphere in which creativity can thrive. The role of leaders in this process is rather crucial, because leaders can promote positive morale and levels of engagement through their ability to listen to and review their feedback.

The other important aspect in increasing engagement is the recognition and reward of employee achievements. Recognition may take place in various forms, such as at individual meetings or more institutionalized programs of recognition. The important way to go is to make sure the recognition is practical and that it fits into the value system of the organization. By letting employees know that their efforts are valued and that they will help the company achieve success, the employees will feel more likely to stay loyal and driven.

Opportunities for professional development are also very critical in improving engagement. Companies that invest in training and development make it known to employees that they are important to the company and that their development matters. This not only benefits the area of the enhancement of skills but also in areas of career progression, which can greatly increase the satisfaction and retention of employees. Clearly defined career ladders and the possibilities of acquiring new skills can make employees feel that they are part of the future of the organization.

Besides, it is critical to create a workplace atmosphere that facilitates work-life balance. Flexible working arrangements- this can help an employee balance life and work by ensuring they use available flexible working arrangements, like remote working or flexible hours. Such flexibility may result in more job satisfaction and less burnout, which boils down to increased engagement.

The inclusion of technology would also facilitate engagement activities. Technologies that allow communication and collaboration can be used to fill the distance between remote and in-office employees and make everyone feel like a member of the team. Also, the adoption of data analytics to understand patterns of engagement and areas that need improvement can be very helpful. Feedback about the employees and their performance can be analyzed, and this can help the organizations improve their engagement approaches in order to suit the needs of their employees.

Lastly, promoting a feeling of purpose and connection to the mission of the organization could be of great benefit to creating engagement. Employees are motivated by a sense of relevance; that is, they become excited when they realize how their job can positively impact the larger objective of the organization. This necessitates open communication by the leadership of the business on the vision of the company and how an individual employee will play a role in this vision.

Altogether, improving employee engagement involves a complex strategy that comprises free communication, recognition, career development, work-life balance, use of technology, and a sense of purpose. In emphasizing the above areas, organizations will be able to develop an environment in which a worker feels appreciated and concerned, leading to the success and innovativeness of the business.

Developing Training Programs

Designing quality training can enable teams to excel in the art of making quick decisions, which is increasingly becoming a prerequisite to succeed in the current business environment. Implementation of such programs necessitates a needs-based, multifaceted, yet flexible plan that can be designed to accommodate rapidly changing requirements of each department and their respective skill sets in an organization.

The successful training program is based on its structure. It must be modular, which means it should be customized depending on the roles within the department in which one is knowledgeable. The modularity would allow every participant to view content that concerns them in their everyday activities and duties. An example would be to provide onboarding sessions with new users on basic ideas and prompt writing basics. In contrast, experienced users would be introduced to more advanced work on complex prompt optimization and strategic use.

Practical examples and practical tasks are the essential elements of these training modules. The focus of the challenges is to simulate actual business challenges. As a result, participants are able to apply learning within a controlled environment, making it easier to understand how prompt engineering can be used to leverage outcomes in the context of the business. Samples of these exercises may involve writing scripts of sales letters, creation of customer service messages or drafts, and creation of a marketing material. All these practical exercises do not only improve the learning process but also lead to confidence-boosting experiences as the participants are assured about the benefits of their skills.

Incentives to inform and reward proficiency may be in the form of certification systems. These may include digital badges to show the completion of particular modules as well as internal certifications to acknowledge advanced proficiency in prompt engineering methods. These systems are used as a motivation tool to ensure that continuous learning and development of skills are facilitated. Besides, they offer a uniform index of competence which can be taken note of throughout the company.

Constant learning is another leg of successful training schemes. Technology is changing; therefore, the skills and knowledge of the people who adopt it must change as well. Regular refreshers, microlearning modules, and peer teaching opportunities must also be added to their training calendar so that the teams can be up to date with scheduled, timely engineering innovations. This continuous learning keeps the level of proficiency and flexibility high, which is very important as new values and techniques come up.

Moreover, establishing an interactive learning environment will make training some of its programs more effective. To introduce the concept of best practices, promoting cross-departmental workshops and collaborative projects will help to share ideas. Not only does it expand the horizon of prompt engineering as applied to various business environments, but it also develops a cohesive culture of innovation and problem-solving.

Last but not least, as a continuous training step, internal prompt playbooks may be developed and propagated. Such playbooks are considered a store of knowledge, where standard templates, model prompts, and troubleshooting are stored. They facilitate the retention of uniformity of immediate use and serve as a good reference tool to various employees, new and experienced ones alike. By ensuring that these playbooks are readily available and kept up-to-date, organizations will be able to maintain a high degree of agility and quickly available expertise in engineering across all of the teams.

In the strict sense, engineering of timely training is about creating an effective system that contributes to learning and application, as well as to further improvement. It is all about making teams armed with the capabilities to take advantage of AI to drive business success through innovation and efficiency.

Monitoring HR Metrics

When it comes to the human resource field, tracking and assessing metrics is crucial to business success. The HR metric landscape is immense, covering multiple areas, giving a glimpse of workforces, the health or an organization, and its overall strategic direction. An important aspect of this monitoring process is careful collation and analysis of data relating to recruitment, employee engagement, retention, and performance management.

The recruitment funnel is one of the key measures of HR performance as it monitors the efficiency and effectiveness of the recruitment process. The metric requires examination of the number of prospects through the hiring process at every step, whether it is at the application point, at the final offer stage, and so on. By tracking these steps, HR professionals can detect bottlenecks and improve their recruitment strategies in a way that attracts top talent more efficiently.

The other important metric is staff engagement, which will provide ideas on how committed employees are to their work and the organization. Communication, surveys, feedback, and observation are some of the methods that measure this metric. A high engagement rate is usually synonymous with high productivity, low turnover rates, and higher morale. As such, employee engagement is a strategic concern for HR.

Employees are monitored according to retention rates in order to get a picture of workforce stability and satisfaction. Turnover rates are expensive and disruptive, and are usually an indication of problems within the company. Based on the turnover data, human resources can devise ways of boosting retention, such as improving the workplace culture, providing better benefits/remuneration, and other methods of career development.

The metrics involved in performance management are concerned with the measurement of the productivity and effectiveness of employees. This is achieved by developing performance expectations, reviewing them regularly, and offering useful criticism. Performance measures assist in understanding those who perform particularly well, and hence they might qualify to be promoted, and those who are not performing well, so as to unlock mechanisms of change through training.

One more value that has become of utmost importance is the analysis of diversity and inclusion metrics. These measures evaluate the population of different demographic groups within the organization and allow checking that the diversity program works. The diverse opinions and experiences that organizations have brought about through the establishment of an inclusive workplace may result in innovative solutions and a more harmonious workplace.

In order to track these HR metrics effectively, organizations have to opt for advanced analytics tools and a dashboard. The tools claim to offer real-time data visualization, a factor that allows HR departments to make appropriate decisions fast. Dashboards can track trends over a period of time, compare measures to industry standards and forecast future staffing requirements.

Besides, incorporating AI and machine learning apps will correct and improve the precision and speed of HR measurements. Such technologies can automate data collection and help identify patterns and predictive insights, enabling an HR professional to make strategic decisions instead of working with manual labor.

To conclude, the process of monitoring HR measures should be complex and demand high-tech and strategic approaches. Through proper analysis of these metrics, organizations can be in a position to streamline their workforce management practices, increase employee satisfaction, and further achieve business success. The continued examination and redesign of the HR metrics will make sure that the organization will be responsive and flexible to both internal and external changes in the business environment.

CHAPTER 14

CONCLUSION AND CALL TO ACTION

Recap of Key Points

The principle of leveraging AI for business, as she has explained, pertains to the already mentioned concept of prompt engineering. This concept, described as writing clear rules for AI systems, is central to establishing real business gains. It comprehensively lays out the postulates of the science of prompt engineering, its role, and responsibilities that are more than technical implementation. It is a business tactic that can go hand in hand with different functions in an organization, like marketing, sales, and operations.

The story highlights the developments of large language models (LLMs) and their disruptive possibilities in the business. Companies can now use GPT-3 and GPT-4 to optimize productivity and further develop their development. The book states these models as essential instruments of digital transformation and provides a historical background that links technological achievements with the present demands in the market.

In setting out the anatomy of effective business prompts, this text offers a solid overview of what goes into making a prompt successful. This entails the designation of roles, explicit definition of tasks, background information, and format requirements. The focus is on detail and clarity, and this is what is needed to produce meaningful business outcomes. By proposing the concepts of prompt variables and modularity, the book provides a vision of prompt development as reusable and adaptable preliminary templates that have the potential to be utilized in any number of business situations.

This book also clears myths and misconceptions about prompt engineering. It refutes the belief that prompt engineering is a domain of technical specialists, demonstrating with the help of case studies how such tasks can be completed by non-technical teams working in the field of HR, marketing, and so forth. It also removes the fear of AI as a black box, and then it indicates that early tuning and validation should be implemented to monitor and improve the outputs of AI.

The other important point discussed is the alignment of the AI capabilities with the business objectives. It notes distinct features in which AI can be superior to humans, e.g., summarizing, classifying, but it also recognizes that human supervision is needed where human judgment is vital. This neutral opinion is useful in tempering expectations about the use of AI in the business.

The latter parts of the book are devoted to how to construct good prompts that are aligned with business outcomes. The steps include reducing complex business issues into promptable tasks, clarity, context, and intent in the prompt construction. Together, the book offers workable examples and structures to assist businesses in ordering prompts in such a manner that they are precise and outcome-focused.

In general, the book can be useful to business people as it guides them in overcoming the complexity of prompt engineering. It teaches readers about the knowledge and tools necessary to build an effective culture of innovation and continuous improvement in business processes through the integration of AI. The reader can also understand what they can do with those ideas and models. I would encourage the reader to take what they learn and apply it to their unique challenges in business, to drive adoption and measure how prompt engineering results in organizational success.

Empowering Business Leaders

In the fast-changing world of artificial intelligence, entrepreneurs find themselves on the brink of a new dawn where their knowledge and application of prompt engineering can totally change the way their businesses operate. This chapter explores how business leaders may become decisively empowered by adopting and mastering the art of prompt engineering, which is the ability to put together concise instructions that can guide AI to provide business-relevant insights.

Business leaders today are faced with not only the challenge of having to negotiate the complex market environments they find themselves in, but also having to consider integrating technological advancements that are capable of providing a competitive advantage. The allusion to prompt engineering appears as an instrument that can close the divide between the traditional business processes and progressive potentialities of AI. By understanding how to do this, leaders will be able to improve decision-making processes and smooth operations, and eventually contribute to business prosperity.

Among the most influential ways to empower business leaders with the help of prompt engineering is the capability to turn wide-range business goals into concrete and definite AI tasks. This would be a process of simplifying too large business issues into small, manageable issues that AI can readily and effectively deal with. To illustrate, a business objective related to more efficient customer service can be converted into prompts that auto-remind answer creation, auto-classification of customer requests, and auto-prioritization of support tickets.

Additionally, incorporating prompt engineering into business strategies enables leaders to tailor AI outputs to the organizational goals and values. Such customization is important to make sure that AI-built solutions will not only work but also be effective and in line with both the brand and the expectations of the customers. Leaders are in a position to prescribe parameters in prompts to have AI outputs comply with particular tones, formats, and contexts of business to ensure consistency and relevance.

Another way of empowering business leaders is by ensuring a culture of being able to learn and change. The provision of AI technologies will change, and so will our strategies and competencies of those who lead a business. Leaders are advised to undertake continuous studies, visit industry conferences, and utilize e-copies of current prompt libraries to equip themselves with up-to-date knowledge and know-how of prompt engineering. This proactive approach not only increases their own capacities but also equips their organizations to be highly adaptive and welcoming to new opportunities and to deal with new challenges.

Moreover, the observable engagement of business executives in timely engineering is also that of developing cross-functional coordination internally in firms. By incorporating prompt engineering in different departments, leaders can make sure that interdepartmental efforts between the IT, marketing, and customer service sections will be more synergic. Such integration promotes a stronger alignment in the way their different teams tackle problems and innovate, as they would now have the tools and the algorithms to leverage AI in their fields.

The gist of empowering business leadership with prompt engineering includes giving them the knowledge and tools to utilize AI capabilities to the fullest. It is about the changing leadership working every day to modern standards of dynamic, technical-savvy, and futuristic directions. In this way, not only can leaders become more successful and effective in their work, but they can also stimulate their organizations to sustainable growth and success in the digital age. The chapter can assist the leaders in dealing with this transformational process by providing them with guidance on key insights, strategies, and practices that they can use to make a direct business impact.

Next Steps for Implementation

With organizations on the cusp of implementing quick engineering into their business models, it is a strategic course of action and careful execution. The initial move in this revolutionary process is to state a well-defined set of objectives that support and relate to top-level business objectives. The most important thing is to establish the description of success within the scope of prompt engineering, be it the improved customer relations, newfound operational efficiency, or decision-making effectiveness. This transparency will aid the provision of quick engineering solutions, as they will be able to measure the value of solutions deployed.

Prompt engineering can be integrated into the current business processes and, therefore, requires a joint approach. IT, HR, and operations cross-functional teams must collaborate and come up with essential areas where timely engineering can increase efficiency and innovation. The result of this partnership is that not only does it properly integrate the technology into the organizational structure, but it also promotes a culture of constant assessment and change with new developments in technology.

To enable efficient implementation, the organizations are expected to invest in the construction of an effective prompt library. This means having a centralized place of well-developed prompts that can be accessed and adapted by different departments. A library like this can be an excellent source of help since teams can use already tested prompts that fit their particular needs. This library must be periodically updated and audited to keep things topical and effective as business requirements change and new AI possibilities come along.

Training and development are a crucial part of the successful incorporation of prompt engineering. Prompts creation, implementation, and revision should be the skills of the employees at any level. This could be done by having holistic training processes that look at the technical and the strategic side of prompt engineering. The creation of a learning environment will enable employees to think on their own. It can be prompted to do further revision processes and come up with novel solutions that will help organizations save on work processes.

Further, it is vital to create a feedback cycle to improve the system of prompt engineering. The input of other key stakeholders, such as the end-users and heads of departments, should be analyzed and gathered. The obtained feedback is useful in determining areas to improve, as well as the prompts being subject to frequent changes depending on the dynamics of the business. Moreover, it promotes a participatory method whereby employees are made to feel part of the success of timely engineering projects.

In the endeavor to drive the company towards the timely engineering course, there is a need to track and provide the results. This consists of establishing metrics and KPIs on the success of prompts towards business goals. Consistent reporting not only clarifies the worth of providing timely engineering but also gives information on the areas that need correction or improvement. This openness in the outcomes builds trust and acceptance among stakeholders, opening the door to more investment in AI-enabled methods.

Lastly, it is critical to be dynamic and flexible in the fast-changing AI environment. Organizations need to be aware of recent trends in AI technologies and be ready to adjust their immediate engineering solutions accordingly. This progressive approach also ensures that the organization is able to be at the same level as the other competitors and at the same time be able to take advantage of any new opportunities that might emerge. When businesses incorporate agility into their strategic planning, it will enable them to protect their operations into the future and maintain the ability to prompt engineering to transform their businesses and succeed in the long term.

Looking Forward

With our eyes to the horizon, the sphere of business is to receive a new twist where the emerging discipline of prompt engineering offers a facelift. It is not only the change in the way businesses conduct themselves, but also the fundamental change in resolving problems and innovations. During the next few years, prompt engineering will become one of the most significant aspects of business strategy as it will provide companies with the competitive advantage they need.

The prospect of prompt engineering is its capability to make the process more streamlined, make better decisions, and be more innovative. Through the development of contextual and specific prompts, companies can take advantage of AI and automate complicated processes, minimize the number of mistakes that humans make, and become more efficient. This is especially important as firms continue to seek to adjust to a fast-changing business environment, where speed and flexibility are key success factors.

Besides, the contribution of prompt engineering to data-driven decision-making cannot be underestimated. Companies are flooded with massive quantities of data, and the process of rapidly refining this data into business insights is of tremendous value. Immediate engineering allows the development of the AI prompts to crunch through data, analyze patterns, and deliver scaled-down and relevant reports. This not only assists in strategic planning but also enables businesses to react before the market changes and consumer demands.

With businesses adopting AI in their operations, the issue of maintaining ethics and compliance will become more paramount. Prompt engineering offers a methodology of intra-procedural integration of these considerations into the workflow of AI, such that the results remain regulatorily compliant and ethically sound. By integrating guardrails and human-in-the-loop systems, companies can curb the risks posed by AI, including biases and data privacy issues, protecting their reputation and gaining the confidence of their consumers.

The future of prompt engineering is also that of an exchange and continuous learning. As the AI technologies develop, the abilities and methods of those who use them have to evolve, as well. Companies will have to cultivate an innovative mindset, where risks are taken and the lessons learnt by taking risks, as well as making mistakes, are part and parcel of growing. This involves investing in training modules to improve the swift engineering competence of their employees and by developing an ambiance that facilitates solution-orientation.

Along with it, the implementation of prompt engineering into business practices will require cross-functional cooperation. IT, HR, and operations will have to collaborate to streamline the implementation of AI tools toward business goals. Such a collaborative methodology will become essential in creating AI solutions that are not only technically effective but also not contradictory to the strategic view of that organization.

Moving forward, the discerning businesses of the future will emerge out of those who can embrace the capability of timely engineering to grow on ethical and prompt engineering efficiency and innovation. Incorporating prompt engineering into the very silhouette of their operations, businesses will be able to stay in the limelight of the latest technological achievements and remain flexible enough to satisfy the changing demands of their customers. Such proactive measures not only precondition the businesses on a path to success but also clear the path towards a future where AI as a respected companion introduces business excellence.

EPILOGUE

As we close the pages of "Prompt Engineering for Business Success," the narrative of AI's transformative potential in the corporate world is far from over. The insights provided in this playbook are designed to serve as a catalyst, sparking innovation and driving strategic advancements across industries. The landscape of business is ever-evolving, and the tools and strategies discussed here are meant to equip leaders and professionals with the confidence to harness AI's power effectively.

Throughout this book, we have explored the art and science of crafting precise prompts those critical inputs that unlock the vast capabilities of AI. From enhancing productivity with automated solutions to driving growth through strategic AI deployments, the applications are as varied as the challenges they address. The methodologies outlined offer a structured approach to integrating AI, ensuring that it is not merely an add-on but a core component of business strategy.

The stories and examples shared underscore the importance of adapting to new technologies with agility and foresight. By embedding AI into daily operations, businesses can achieve unprecedented levels of efficiency and innovation. However, the journey does not end here. The realm of AI is continuously expanding, and staying ahead requires ongoing learning and adaptation.

This book encourages its readers to become pioneers in their fields, leveraging AI not just as a tool but as a partner in innovation. By fostering a culture of experimentation and embracing the potential for safe failures, organizations can cultivate an environment where creativity thrives and new ideas are constantly tested and refined.

As you step into the future of AI-driven business, let this playbook be your guide. Embrace the frameworks and strategies discussed, adapt them to your unique context, and continue to explore the endless possibilities that prompt engineering offers. With these tools at your disposal, the potential for saving time, boosting productivity, and growing your career is limitless. May this be the beginning of an exciting and rewarding venture into the realm of AI-powered business success.

www.ingramcontent.com/pod-product-compliance
Lightning Source LLC
Chambersburg PA
CBHW070930210326
41520CB00021B/6868